Must be Present to Win

to Win

Doug Sterbenz and Paul Heagen

First published by Dog Ear Publishing
4011 Vincennes Rd
Indianapolis, IN 46268
www.dogearpublishing.net

dog ear
PUBLISHING

ISBN: 978-1-4575-6308-9

This book is printed on acid-free paper.

Printed in the United States of America

Contents

Note From The Authors

Paul Heagen

When I first started working with Doug, it was to help him refine his leadership model and style in his role as a senior executive in utility operations. However, reflecting my approach and beliefs as a leadership coach, I rummaged around in our talks to uncover some of his own experiences in life, his "story" that has shaped who he is. When you take the time to do that, you often discover that no assessment, no abstract learning model is as instructive or impactful as simply knowing your own story. We become students of ourselves and thus, students of others who have their own stories.

The stories in this book are all drawn from those explorations together. Sure, there are many other stories of other leaders we could have included, but the real point was to encourage you to understand just how much is already in you when it comes to being an authentic, present leader. You don't have to try to be like someone else; you just have to be a great version of who you are.

Doug Sterbenz

When I first started working with Paul, I was mostly interested in picking up some tips on leadership, but he pestered me with questions about my life, work experiences, memories as a kid and even my dad. What's that got to do with anything? As it turns out, it had everything to do with everything. The notion of Leaders Must Be Present To Win® came out of one of those stories and has now served as the seminal message to what I had wanted to get into words and share with others for so long.

My work with Paul was transformational for me. It got me out of my world of data and facts and processes so I could really embrace the need to connect with people on a deeper level to have the impact I wanted to have. I would encourage all of you to consider having a coach in your life—not just a friend, but a coach with the skills of someone like Paul—to prod, poke, challenge and encourage you to become something more than you might on your own. He has done that for me, and my passion now is to help others do the same, through my talks and this book.

"We often fail to be present because, honestly, we have been juiced to believe something way more interesting lies just over the hill."

"Many people sign up for leadership. Few show up. Leaders who are present, win, along with those they lead and those they follow."

Foreword

Time is not on your side.

We talk about having time for this, time for that. Making time. Taking time. Saving time. Borrowing time.

However, the reality of our stimulus-saturated world today is that with so much coming at us, we never seem to have enough time. Mastering time—as opposed to it ruling over you—seems a quaint notion in an era when we feel compelled or oppressed to fit everything into the scarce time we have.

We pay a price. It is subtle, but it erodes one of the most crucial areas of leadership.

We are no longer in the moment.

It's trendy right now to talk about being "in the moment" but what does that mean? Being "in the moment"—concentrating fully and singularly on what is in front of us or on our minds—seems a fanciful quest, one that creates enormous tension with our need to be efficient, to move, to make the most of...time.

We can't be "here" if we are somewhere else.

We are no longer present.

We see it all around us. The person in the meeting who cannot resist glancing at text messages. Interrupting to finish others' sentences so we can move on to something else. Skimming through operations reports or business plans without seeing the real promise or perils. Failing to slow down long enough to ask that extra question that just might unearth an idea, a hidden sentiment.

This idea of *presence*—where we are connected with what is going on around us, with the people in our space, even wired into what is being said or happening—is key to leadership. However, the fact that we have to work so hard to develop and sustain that sense of presence should worry us.

We can't be "here" if we are somewhere else.

Research has made it strikingly clear that there is no such thing as multi-tasking. Oh, we may flit from one thought to another, or one activity to another, even pretend to have one conversation with a person while another one rages in our heads, but we are fooling ourselves. The neural pathways in our brains are fairly narrow roads, and most have developed deep ruts. To move from Point A to Point B—whether that is in some conceptual thinking, finishing a sentence once started, or simply to connect the dots in what we observe in our lives—takes concentrated effort.

When we are "there" instead of "here" at those times, we create some serious cross traffic to those pathways, a demolition derby of activity that is bound to end up in a wreck, sooner or later.

We embrace the virtue of being present, but it wars against our allegiance to outside stimulus. To be present in the ways we will talk about in this book takes time. When time and our use of it is at such a premium, we will find little impetus to be present unless we actively choose it. Over the years, we have sought to reconcile this conflict with books such as *The One-Minute Manager* that assuaged our guilt about busyness and assured us we could connect in deep ways and still keep pace with that ticking clock in our head. Nonsense.

> When time and our use of it is at such a premium, we will find little impetus to be present unless we actively choose it.

We often fail to be present because, honestly, we have been juiced to believe something way more interesting lies just over the hill. All day long, a variety of stimuli continually jacks us up: alerts on our smart phones, instant text messages that feign urgency, streaming headlines. As a consequence, we have little tolerance for things that, at first glance, don't seem that interesting.

The sad reality is that we are losing the war. We can't save time anyway, right? But what we are losing is much more substantial. We are losing the human connection that remains essential to how we make decisions, the relationships we build and the impact we can have as leaders.

My co-author Doug understands first hand this contrast between needing to get things done and being present. A hard-driving, efficient senior operating officer for a multi-billion-dollar electric utility, Doug knew how to accomplish tasks. He could punch through a punch list like nobody else. However, he wanted to learn how to better articulate the principles that had been instilled in him over the years by mentors and friends, to project better as a leader. So he sought my help as a coach.

Back when we first began working together, Doug would whirl from one idea to another, impatient to move on to the next coaching activity or discussion once we had covered the one we were working on to the level of what he would call "good enough."

Doug's approach began to flip when he realized that when he was up on stage—initially speaking to employees or trade groups on behalf of his company and later as the public speaker he has become—he had to *connect*. And to connect meant he had to be *present*. And to be present, he had to slow down and be relentless about being in the moment.

I designed coaching sessions to help Doug experience what it meant to be in the moment, fully invested in that time and space in his thinking, his emotions and even how he reflected that in his physical bearing. What Doug accomplished utilizing this approach was amazing. Over time, stories from his experiences began to pour out. When he shared those stories with me, I slowed him down and mined them for their full worth. Doug learned how to go back in the moment of those experiences and bring them forward today to show others how they can slow down themselves and feel what it's like to be present—physically, mentally and emotionally—in their lives and jobs.

In this book, we share those stories and principles with you to challenge you to be present in ways you never imagined you could. Most chapters will start with a story by Doug, followed by some reflections by me as a leadership coach. A mix of story and theory, if you will, because we believe for you to truly understand what it means to be present, you need to experience it. Ultimately, we want you to see how crucial being present is to your leadership effectiveness and the impact you can have on others.

The fair question to ask right now—and yes, this is early—is whether you are serious. I mean, dead serious. This book is not just about picking up some new management trick, a few pointers, or something you will plug-and-play with how you lead today. There are countless books out there on strategy, vision, execution—oh, and yes, time management. While these leadership qualities are important, we believe the most effective way to lead people is to be fully present, which means your presence is part of who you are, not just something you do. In my 20 years of coaching senior executives, I am fiercely convinced this is what people want from you. What you have to decide is if this is something you want from yourself.

Presence is part of who you are, not just something you do.

Are you tired of missing ideas?

Are you yearning to get "on the floor" and really experience the pulse of your business?

Are you so crazed keeping up that you've lost track of how to spend real time with people and understand them, and they you?

Are you ready to get out of the squirrel cage and be the kind of leader people feel they know and trust?

Do you have your own stories about how being totally in the moment has had an impact on you and others, or is time just slipping by?

If you answered yes to any of those questions, this book is for you.

The concept of being present is practically extinct, yet has never been more needed in leadership. If you understand and vigorously live out this idea of being present, it can transform your effectiveness. It can magnify your influence. It can change lives, including your own.

If you want to win the war over the most effective use of your time, you must take it head on.

Chapter 1

The Raffle

Someone's got your number; it might as well be YOU.

In my hometown, 50 years years ago, a man by the name of Willard Noller started a Ford dealership.

After running the business successfully for many years, Willard handed the business over to his son Laird. Now his grandsons are being groomed to run the company. They've already beat formidable odds—fewer than 10 percent of family-owned businesses make it to the third generation.

Laird Noller wanted to do something really special to mark that 50-year milestone, so he came up with a big idea. Any person who showed up at the dealership could register for a chance to win a new automobile—a Ford F-150 pickup, a car or an SUV. This was a big deal.

How big? More than 6,000 people visited the dealership in the weeks before the event and filled out one of those little blue tickets in hopes their name would be drawn. A thousand of them showed up the day of the drawing. They all stood in the parking lot underneath the circus tent, eating free hot dogs and chips, waiting to see if this was their lucky day.

Laird himself walked up to the stage and opened the lid to that basket containing 6,000 little blue tickets. He pulled one out and announced the name, "Miles Henderson." Everyone looked around for Miles, expecting him to be jumping up and down, hooting and hollering. But it was quiet. Nobody was jumping up and down. Nobody was celebrating.

Laird called out the name again, this time a little louder, but still no response.

Then Laird did something that made your heart sink for that Miles fellow. Laird tossed the ticket onto the stage, reached back into that basket, drew a new ticket and read that name. Actually, he repeated that action *ten more times* before someone in the crowd finally hollered out "Winner" and drove home in a new Ford Edge.

Now, I ask you, what does a car raffle have to do with a leadership book?

In a benefit raffle, participants write their name on the raffle ticket and drop it into the basket. In this particular raffle, more than 6,000 people put their name on a raffle ticket in hopes of winning. But only about a thousand people showed up for the drawing. They all knew the rules, but the majority still did not show up.

6,000 people put their name on a raffle ticket ... only a thousand showed up.

While it is exciting that someone won that car, we can't help but feel some sympathy for poor Miles, and perhaps the other nine people who missed their chance. After all, it was his name they called. So, why was his ticket tossed to the floor?

The reason was right there on the sign when people registered. It's the rule of almost every raffle:

"You must be present to win."

This notion has come back to me in such a fresh, meaningful way as I reflect on a career that started on the "shop floor" of a power plant and culminated in the executive suite as the COO of a major electric utility. When I look back to the things I sought to represent in my leadership—and where the losses and the wins were, not just for me, but for the people I led—it almost always came down to this notion of being "present."

Must Be Present
To Win

Present. The word has so many—and sometimes confusing or contradictory—meanings.

One of those definitions is pretty disappointing:

Have you ever been part of or observed a roll call vote at a city council or legislative session when someone opts out of taking a stand and just says "Present!" when their name is called? They are acknowledging their presence, but certainly not engaging on the issue at hand. In that case, "present" means nothing more than a warm body taking up a chair.

The other definition is one that certainly feels more encouraging:

This other meaning of "present" (or presently) means "in the moment" or "happening now." Not soon, or sometime, or eventually, but *now*.

If you combine those two meanings, being present means being *fully* engaged and committed in a particular moment.

Being present is harder than it sounds. We are flooded with distractions, pressures on our time and the buzz that competes for our attention. The market is stuffed with books that will assuage you into thinking that the volume of activity you manage is evidence of your leadership, and that the path to effectiveness lies in efficiency. Just so you know, this is not one of those books.

Being present will require you to
go against the current tide and
devote – yes, *devote* –
your time and attention
in a different way.

I love a subtext of Doug's story: Numerous torn ticket
stubs landed on the asphalt parking lot of that dealership before they found a winner. Those tickets represent
something of value, but the value is only realized if you
are there when it matters. A lot of squandered value
ended up on that floor.

A lot of people—about 85 percent of those who had
signed up for that raffle—found something else that
was more important than showing up that day. Maybe
they forgot, maybe they weren't confident in their
chances, maybe they didn't care anymore. They may not
have won anyway, but by not being present, they sure
guaranteed they would lose. They never had a chance to
win.

Similarly, countless people sign up to be leaders. Many
of those people who sign up for leadership simply don't
show up. The saddest part is that unlike that car raffle
where the absent ticket holders were the ones who lost,
when you don't show up as a leader, your people lose.
Your organization loses.

Show Up

In the pages to come, we are going to explore the concept of being present further and more deeply than you might find elsewhere because we believe this leadership quality has not only been overlooked but has also taken on an urgent role in a world where we are just too busy to be much of anywhere, even in our heads.

Part of that deeper dive we will make explores another dimension of being present: *presence*. Defining presence can be elusive, but we know it when we see it or sense it. Presence almost has a spiritual or mystical quality about it, but it goes beyond the limits of someone just taking up space. Presence relates more to the impact you have or the influence you bring to bear. People know when you are in the room.

People know when you are in the room.

My executive coach (yes, leadership coaches should also have a coach of their own if they truly believe in their craft) says it this way: "Leadership is not just about getting things done, but it is about what people become when they are in your presence."

In the next few chapters—through Doug's rich stories and my reflections as a leadership coach over many years—we will reveal exactly what it means to be present and why it is the key factor in winning.

So grab your ticket.

Must
Be Present
To Win

Chapter 2
Physically Present

There really is a "there" there.

 **Graduations are a big deal in our family, especially college graduations.**

A few months before my daughter's college graduation, she called home to discuss the plans for the celebration. She was talking to her mother and me on speakerphone. Admittedly, I wasn't paying much attention, as the conversation centered on punch bowls, party treats and invitations.

In the midst of that conversation, my daughter asked a question that stopped me in my tracks. She asked, "Are grandma and grandpa going to make it to my graduation?"

Before they retired, my mom and dad lived close to us and were always active in our kids' lives. Even now that they've moved out of state, they still stay in touch and communicate regularly with us and our kids. My mom has one of those old-fashioned flip phones, but she can text and send pictures to the grandkids, which she thinks is pretty cool. Not my dad. If you want to talk to him, there is no texting, email or cell phones. You're going to go to his house and knock on the door. He'll talk as long as you want, but it's going to be face-to-face. My kids just don't have the opportunity to see their grandparents in person as much as they used to, so this graduation brought all that longing to the surface in a big way. Once my daughter had grabbed my attention with that question, the importance of their appearance at this event really sank in.

My parents are still in good health, but they really don't travel much anymore. I had mentioned the graduation to them, but honestly did not press it much, knowing the burden it would place on them to make it there.

Not wanting my daughter to be disappointed on her big day, but harboring some anxious doubts about the feasibility of my parents being able to make the trip, I just told her, "They said they'd try to make it." (We fathers can come up with the most carefully crafted ambiguities when we are covering for the fact we haven't the slightest idea what to do!)

The Big Day

Graduation day arrived and we made our way into the gymnasium, found a seat up in the bleachers and waited for the ceremony to start.

Eventually, a sea of black caps and gowns washed like waves into the back of the gymnasium. About halfway through that procession, I saw my daughter, but she hadn't seen us yet. Her eyes scanned the bleachers. Then she saw us—her mom and me—and smiled at us because she expected to see us there.

She took a few more steps and continued to scan the audience, rather intently this time. I could see her brow start to drop and her smile fade a little. I knew what she was looking for. I knew who she was looking for. She continued to scan the crowd, now with more than a hint of resignation.

Then her face lit up. There they were, Grandma and Grandpa, right there on those bleachers. You could see her spirits lift. I swear she stopped walking, rose out of her heels and floated up that center aisle. Her grandma and grandpa were there, physically present!

She knew this was a big day. She was so proud of herself for attaining a college degree when deep down she had doubts that she could. But with her grandma and grandpa making the effort to be there for her that day, her accomplishment became huge.

They were physically present, and it totally rocked her world.

I think you already know what my mom and dad knew—the value of being physically present.

You just had to be there.

"You just had to be there."

That's what you hear from some-one coming back from a spectacu-lar experience, an adventure, a vacation to some exotic locale, a sporting event or a concert.

Being there is an immersion of the senses—sight, sound, touch, smell, taste—that exposes us to stimuli that can never be imagined fully in our minds or cap-tured on a screen or a piece of paper.

Our bodies are wired for physical stimuli; it is how we connect viscerally to the world around us. Being "there"—taking in all those sensory inputs—rivets memories into our heads that can last a long time and even change us.

Our bodies are wired for physical stimuli.

The same can be true for the people who meet you.

In an organizational context, physical presence can easily be discounted in an era when more people work virtu-ally, networked by technology but not by personal prox-imity. According to Gallup Research, some 37 percent of workers now telecommute several days a month. That equates to four times the number who did so 20 years ago. On a broader scale, an increasingly larger number of businesses and their operations are firmly planted on soil in major commercial markets in Western Europe, Asia and South America. However, what really drives globalization today is the growth in emerging markets. Research by McKinsey Global Institute predicts that 40 percent of global growth over the next 15 years will come from 400 midsize emerging-market cities.

We are really spread out.

Advances in technology, operating platforms, visibility into programs and supply networks, and real-time monitoring and control of processes and activity enables and even prompts the increased dispersion of workforces today. All of these elements have contracted the world and demolished many of the physical barriers that have stood in the way of boundary-less business growth. IBM, with a global workforce the size of Cleveland, as far back as 2009 had 40% of its employees working from home. (Hold that thought.) Gallup surveys show that about 25% of all employees work from home all or part of the time.

Except for one thing.

Nearly every recognized employee engagement survey persistently points out that employees want to see management—certainly their direct boss, but also executive management—all the way to the CEO or managing director. This fact has never really changed over decades of such surveys. People want to feel connected to upper management and they want upper management to understand the issues they face in their jobs.

Why does it still matter so much?

Feel the Connection

Some of the reasons are obvious:

PHYSICAL PRESENCE INVITES DIALOGUE

It allows employees to gain an understanding of you as a person and serves as a bit of a field trial in terms of your credibility and poise that only comes from looking someone in the eye. That earlier example of IBM's distributed workforce? As we write this, IBM—which had been saving $100 million in office expenses each year with their work-from-home policy—is reversing course and calling people back to "co-location" centers. Why? Because gains in productivity were coming at the expense of innovation, idea-sharing, teamwork and culture. There is something about being in physical proximity that matters, and management is no exception.

PHYSICAL PRESENCE REPRESENTS A COMMITMENT OF TIME AND ENERGY

It demonstrates that the walk around the shop floor, the design lab, the operations center, the loading docks and the back-office cubicles is more important—at least in that moment—than everything else back in the office. Our priorities are measured by our place in the time/space continuum and what we do with it while we are there. Done well, management of that continuum telegraphs the value we place on the people we meet.

PHYSICAL PRESENCE OFFERS A CONCOMITANT BENEFIT.

At the executive leadership level, it can be hard to get to the truth. The higher you are in executive management, the more likely that people will try to curry favor with you by protecting you (or themselves) from hard realities. As one client of mine once said when he was promoted to CEO, "As of today, I will know less about what's really going on in my business than I ever did before."

Physical Presence and the Role of Sensing

So, how do you make sure you are hearing, seeing and staying in touch with what's going on in your business? The answer is in the question—your senses. Consider those senses: hearing, seeing, touch, smell and taste. They are designed to allow your brain to take in information for what it is, unfiltered and unjudged. We can't pretend that something doesn't taste like it does or sound like it does. What we see is what we get. Touch a hot stove, and you can pretend all you want that it's cold, but it's not. In a larger context, our senses are designed to protect us, to keep us in sync with the world around us and give us reliable signals on how to respond.

We take this most basic human capability—trusting our senses to tell us the truth—and yet we often betray these truths or seek to edit reality in our business or personal lives. Why is that?

We think before we sense.

Thinking, by its very nature, is a re-ordering, evaluation and reprocessing of what is in our heads. The brain's ability to sort, consider, connect and re-frame massive volumes of data points is truly astounding. Yet, when you are trying to be present—especially physically— thinking has to wait its turn. When we set up our critical thinking mechanisms too early, we block inputs that are unwelcome, not easily understood or contrary to our beliefs or experience.

Truth is truth; we cannot edit it to suit ourselves. To be physically present is to inhale all of those inputs with curiosity and without judgment.

Being physically present allows you to leverage your senses to gain insights into your business that may not show up in those executive operations reviews or even dashboard tracking systems.

Leverage your senses to gain insights into your business.

Sensing In Action

Many years ago I flew down to Bentonville, Arkansas, with the CEO of a major food products company to meet with the CEO of Wal-Mart. On our way back to the airport, we stopped at one of his company's restaurants and ordered an item that was new on the menu. My travel companion didn't identify himself as the CEO of the company, nor did they recognize him. As we were leaving, he shook his head and wondered out loud, "The woman behind the counter didn't seem very happy about my order. I wonder what that was all about?"

He spun on his heel and went right back in. After identifying himself as the CEO, he used a bit of charm and honest curiosity to get her talking about why she had been downcast when taking our order.

"We hate it!" she finally admitted. "Your product people just come up with this stuff and never ask us how hard it will be to prepare it."

The next thing we knew, that CEO was back in the kitchen, donning an apron and getting schooled on the problem. You could see the glow on the faces of the workers as he attentively listened to their complaints and suggestions.

You could see the glow on the faces of the workers.

It wasn't long before another menu item replaced that one—one that was a lot easier to prepare.

That single visit had an immediate impact on product development, but more importantly, that specific restaurant experienced a boost in morale because employees felt like they mattered. Neither of those things would have happened if the only experience that CEO had with that restaurant was just a number on a spreadsheet. I know from the plane ride home that he was scolding himself for having been out of touch with that part of the business and was already stirring up ideas about how to involve field operations workers in product testing.

While factors such as technology, real-time management systems, *et al.* do shorten the learning curves and accelerate the flow of information, we have yet to find a way to obviate the human factors—the energy, passion, honesty and mutual respect—that only arise from face-to-face interaction. All the systems, processes, training and workflow management models can do is facilitate efficiency and productivity. What lights up a brand, what makes people believers and what gives them a sense of their role in a larger mission is "being there."

You Must be Present to Win. Physically.

Leaders Must be Present to Win. Physically.

My dad was a fireman, which was pretty cool on those "Bring Your Dad To School" days. While the other kids brought engineers, accountants and maybe a utility executive, I brought a fireman! Being a fireman meant that my dad worked 24 hours on and 24 hours off. He spent every other night away from home, and away from me.

On the days when he was at the fire station, I'd ride my bike across town just to be with him. We would spend our time at the station working on some kind of project. We would refinish old furniture, fix something that was broken or work on a car.

On the days when he was not at the fire station, he was usually working a part-time job painting or roofing. I helped him on those jobs, too. My earliest memories involve working with my dad, either at the fire station or somewhere else.

We had a relationship built on work. That's how he taught me life's lessons. Some fathers teach their kids through words; he taught me through work. If I stayed out a little too long at night doing something I shouldn't have been doing, I didn't get a lecture. My dad would just flip on the light in my bedroom and tap the edge of the bed with his foot a little earlier in the morning than normal. We would work a little harder and a little longer than the day before. I got the message.

We had a relationship built on work.

My dad is a wiry, tough, scrappy man with skin like leather from working in the sun. He could scale a roof like a squirrel and could lay shingles fast and straight.

During the summer between my junior and senior year of high school, a huge hail storm hit our city. Nearly every roof in town needed to be replaced, and many houses needed to be repainted. My Dad was busy roofing and I was busy painting every day that summer. The painting and roofing business was good, but it was hard work for both of us.

That summer, I found myself wanting to do more things for him, not because he asked—he was not a man of many words—but because I wanted to. My dad's knees were bad. He could lay the shingles on the roof just fine, but he had a hard time carrying the heavy shingles up the ladder.

Most days, I would get up extra early and go to the place where my dad would be roofing for the day. By the early light of dawn, I would carry those bundles of shingles up onto the roof for a couple of hours before going to my painting job. At the end of the day, I would stop back by the job site to see if my dad needed any help.

We were both so busy that summer, that my dad and I didn't get to spend much time with each other, usually just crossing paths in the morning or afternoon. But sometimes I would still be carrying shingles when my dad arrived from the fire station to start his roofing job. On those mornings we would find time for short talks up on the roof.

Rooftop Talks

One morning we were up on a roof when the home-owner—a businessman in a suit—walked out onto the driveway and said, "Hi, Bob. How's it going this morning?" They exchanged a few words, and then we watched as he loaded his golf clubs into the trunk of his car and left for work. I looked at my dad, hoping to see some reaction, but he just picked up his roofing hatchet and started to pound nails.

Later that afternoon, I met my dad again on the same roof and we both watched as the businessman pulled into his driveway. This time, he was dressed in golf attire. He removed the golf clubs from his trunk and put them in his garage. He walked back out onto the driveway, exchanged a few pleasant words with my dad and went into his house.

I'll never forget what happened next.

My dad laid his roofing hatchet down, turned to me, looked me straight in the eye and said, "I don't know anything about what that guy does or how he does it. I don't know the first thing about his world, but he sure seems to have an easier life than us. You ought to go try to do what he does, and I think it has something to do with college."

My dad doesn't even remember that talk, but I'll never forget it.

Before that day, I hadn't given much thought to the idea of going to college. Nobody in my family had ever graduated from college. In fact, I didn't personally know any college graduates.

My dad planted a seed that day high up on that businessman's roof. He was able to plant that seed because of his physical presence that day. He covered that seed with a little more hard work that summer. That seed was later watered and fertilized with an unexpected football scholarship to a small junior college. That seed sprouted and took root, eventually growing into an engineering degree and a pretty nice career.

My dad doesn't even remember that talk, but I'll never forget it.

D oug's conversation about what do with his life may not have had anywhere near the same impact if it had happened around the kitchen table as part of a family's normal routine. There is something about sharing the experience of work, getting into the world of the other person, that changes the conversation and its meaning.

What is the real value proposition in this notion of being physically present? Is it an anecdotal feel-good exercise or does it translate into greater performance of an organization? It does "cost" you to be physically present in tangible ways—time and money—so what's the ROI for that?

When you line up the swath of employee engagement surveys available to most businesses today, it is easy to see the thread across all of them: The Human Factor. Sure, the "hard" factors are there—effectiveness of systems, clarity of strategy and market penetration. All of these things matter to people who want to feel they are part of a viable enterprise. However, the inescapable human factors are profoundly shaped by physical presence.

This concept of physical presence has some key elements.

Accessibility

How many of you reading this book have an "open-door policy?"

Most executives will contend that they have open-door policies. But do people wear out the path from where they work to your office? Do they go out of their way to tell you or show you something that you need to see or hear? In all our experience in senior management or leadership coaching, we have never seen a situation where employees felt it was better for them to go to the executive than for the executive to come to them. Maybe it's fear, or natural anxiety or even deference that gives them pause before they cross that threshold.

We believe that part of this reluctance comes from the high value the physical presence your visit to them represents. When you "get out and about" you are no longer on your turf; you are on theirs. And when that's the case, the conversations tend to change. You learn something about them, and they learn something about you.

Accessibility is not just an open door; it is open ears and open minds.

Trust

We all know that being an effective supervisor, manager or leader requires a high level of trust. Trust is chemistry. Trust is art. But trust is also proximal. When you spend time with someone, observe their behaviors, body language and expressions, you get to know them on a deeper level than you would through a note, email or video.

Trust is chemistry. Trust is art.

It's hard to trust somebody who you never see. It's a lot easier to trust somebody that you see often. Being physically present with people builds trust. Lack of physical presence destroys trust.

Communication

Being physically present makes it far more likely that you will communicate with people, but it also means a much greater opportunity for mutual understanding, the real goal of good communication.

When you are physically present and accessible, you get a chance to communicate your mission, your principles, your values and your beliefs in a way that enables your personal passion for them to come through. Too often, we get enamored with the elegance or brilliance of our strategy, plan or vision as if the words alone are sufficient to stir the soul. What gets people to dig deep and rally is when they feel the commitment and energy of management to that vision or strategy. That can only come when you are physically present.

In turn, you can read all the operations reviews and study all the dashboard performance measures, but there's nothing quite like walking the floor to get a true sense of how all of that is working or not working. Asking questions and honestly, patiently listening to the answers helps you read the pulse of your organization.

If businesses today expect to survive and flourish, they must embrace change as a norm. However, that change involves more than just systems and processes; it also includes people's beliefs and behaviors. Communicating by listening and clarifying, by seeking to understand as much as to be understood, is key to that. And that dialogue is only done well when you are fully there in the moment, physically present.

In being physically present, you get to influence and be influenced.

If you want to be accessible, create trust and communicate effectively; be physically present.

Physical Presence

Accessibility
Influence
Trust
Communications

Chapter 3

Mentally Present

Sometimes the brain has a mind of its own.

 Two years into my first professional job as an engineer in a coal-fired power plant, I was promoted to production supervisor.

The technical aspects of the job appealed to me, but I was about to find out about other elements of the job that had not been covered in any book I'd ever read or college course I'd taken to that point.

Sid was the most senior production supervisor in the entire company. He knew the plant like the back of his hand, but he wasn't much for leadership formality. Sid's boss would say, "Sid, you can't let your crew call you disrespectful names like 'Old Man' or 'Pops.'"

However, that informality suited Sid just fine because he just really wanted to be one of the guys anyway. Sid would reply to his boss, "I don't care what they call me, as long as they call me when the coffee is ready."

Don't Ignore Fires

One night, just before shift change, a young, eager new operator rushed into the control room out of breath and burst out, "Sid, I was on the back side of the coal pile and saw some of the coal pile smoldering! It is smoldering pretty good. I think there's a fire! What should we do?"

Fires in a coal power plant are an ugly business. After all, coal is a fuel, and to have a fire smoldering in that heap presents some serious challenges. In those instances, it's often hard to find the source of the fire because smoke seeps out from everywhere. It likely has spread to more than one location, and putting it out means dragging that coal pile in all directions to separate the unburned coal from the embers, or dousing it with water that can put that coal out of business for a few days while it dries out.

You don't ignore coal pile fires.

Except, Sid's shift was just about to end, and an issue like this was bound to keep him on duty for longer than he planned. He looked at his watch, turned to the young man and asked, "Did anybody else see it?"

The young operator said, "No, nobody else has seen the fire! I am the only one that goes back there. It's hard to see, but I was out there making my rounds like they trained me to do and I saw it. It is smoldering pretty good. What should we do?" By this time the young fellow was pretty animated, perhaps even puzzled about why Sid was not reflecting the same urgency.

Sid winked at that young man and said, "Out of sight, out of mind!" and then turned and walked away, leaving the young operator just standing there.

All the energy, the enthusiasm and the passion drained right out of that young man's face and puddled right there on the control room floor. It's hard to imagine him taking the initiative again after an experience like that.

"Out of sight, out of mind!"

How did I know what happened that night at shift change? Because my crew was on schedule to relieve Sid's crew, and I saw the whole thing. What did I do?

Nothing.

Sure, I had my operator go look at it, and he put out the fire when our shift started, but I did not address the real issue. The real leadership issue.

What should I have done? I should have stepped in, but I didn't. What was I thinking?

Maybe that was the problem—I wasn't thinking. I was not mentally present.

True, I did the immediate, correct thing. Essentially, I responded to my training and even a bit of common sense, but what I failed to do in that moment was think critically and to be fully engaged with the entire situation.

Had I done that, the long-term implications of Sid's indifference, its impact on morale or professional diligence, would have been just as apparent to me as the coal fire itself. A bad interaction with a supervisor like that gets talked about in the break room or in the parking lot. Then it gets passed along until it becomes folklore and legend. Before you know it, dozens of people no longer think coal fires matter, or they think that ignoring a problem on your watch is acceptable.

Being mentally present means being alert—absorbing and processing information and making critical decisions in the moment. Oddly enough, though most of us would consider ourselves as having a decent brain, we fail to be mentally present in our work and daily lives.

It happens more than we want to admit.

Runaway Train

On the night of May 13, 2015, an Amtrak train—traveling at twice its assigned speed—hurled off the rails on a curve approaching Philadelphia, killing eight people and injuring 200 others.

Authorities immediately initiated a formal investigation. News media instantly questioned the track conditions, saying that not enough money had been invested on track maintenance. Then they questioned the aging Amtrak infrastructure, arguing that with better train controls, the derailment could have been prevented.

While the crash stirred plenty of debate about infrastructure, investigators still found no mechanical issues that were the culprit. The focus of the investigation then bore down squarely on the engineer at the controls of the train that night. Surely, some speculated, he was working overtime and dozed off, or had drugs in his system, or was suffering from an undisclosed physical ailment, or was neglecting his duty by texting or talking with someone on his cell phone.

It turns out the engineer was a perfectly healthy individual with no drugs or alcohol in his system, and he was not on his cell phone or surfing the Internet while on duty. But he had operated the train that night at twice the rated speed.

How can that happen?

It took a year, but NTSB investigators finally concluded that the engineer had been distracted that night by radio chatter from another train that had been hit by a rock. He was paying attention to those details and simply lost track of where he was, with the 50 MPH-rated curve just ahead.

Oddly enough, the engineer was doing part of his job. A rock hitting a train is a safety issue—perhaps vandals tossing debris from an overpass, or maybe a rock slide. This engineer was not failing to do his work, but the NTSB cited him for losing his situational awareness because of the radio chatter. Essentially, he was not mentally present in paying attention to broader issues amid the more immediate focus of the radio chatter.

On our Watch

Right now, at companies all over the world, leaders are barreling down the tracks at the helm of very important, critical functions, but they are not mentally present. As good as they may be in handling the obvious challenge, it's fair to wonder what they are missing.

What usually suffers is what's on the periphery or the long game.

It's fair to wonder what we are missing.

When you are with your team at work, are you mentally present? At all times? We all have distractions. But I ask you. Is that distraction more important, at that very moment, than what you are actually doing?

Being mentally present means being fully engaged in what is happening at the moment.

The brain is an amazing organ, but sometimes we treat it like it has a mind of its own.

The average human brain is capable of processing at 100,000,000,000,000 —*that's 100 trillion*—operations per second. In case that's not impressive to you, it is about 100,000 times faster than the fastest computer.

The brain represents about three percent of the total body weight of a human but 20 percent of the body's energy.

We use our brains—a lot.

Sometimes our
brain has a mind
of its own.

However, much of that brain use is not even conscious, or at least not active. Just imagine all the synapses assigned to motor movement, balance, breathing and bodily systems. The brain is a sucker for stimuli—the "data" coming in the form of sight, sound, taste, touch and smell. All that stimuli has to be processed and measured against our databases of knowledge, which allows us to associate chocolate with pleasure or high temperatures with danger. Finally, the stimuli organized and directed to either be stored or take action. Daydreaming, let's not forget, takes up part of our mental capacity as well.

Amid all that traffic is the higher order of critical thinking. Even this has its metaphorical "layers"—easy stuff such as writing or speaking, and stuff that's hard, such as identifying patterns in a math puzzle or sorting through a highly complex design.

We are easily distracted from the higher order of critical thinking. It takes an intentional, focused effort to bear down and think deeply, critically and even creatively about the world around us. Like anything you do well, it takes a commitment, practice and discipline for it to become a habit.

Great leaders are present mentally.

Being present mentally involves several key human qualities:

A NATURAL SUSPICION OF THE STATUS QUO

Our bodies, and nature itself, are designed to achieve homeostasis—a stable equilibrium between often conflicting forces or conditions. Successful leaders know that the status quo is the enemy of innovation, organizational change and personal growth. Routine can lull us into complacency, and we too easily turn off our thinking because it seems unneeded to influence our environment. Being mentally present means coming into situations with a wariness toward comfort and satisfaction. A certain pace and rhythm in the business flow is needed, but it can too easily create white noise around some real perils or opportunities. Some intentional disruption has a way of recalibrating the business and exposing what needs to change.

A PERSISTENT CURIOSITY FOR THE UNKNOWN

While suspicion of the status quo involves challenging your situation or conditions, curiosity is rooted in the notion that there is much more we don't know than what we do. Curiosity opens a path of discovery about why things are done the way they are and how they can be better. Mentally present leaders have a great respect for their own ignorance as a way to invite the right conversations and stimulate fresh thinking and ideas.

A RESPECT FOR YOUR SENSES AS MUCH AS YOUR INTELLECT

It may seem counterintuitive to put our five senses ahead of that amazing creation called the brain, but remember that much of the information that is up there came first from the senses: what we read, what we see, what we hear, what we touch. Being mentally present means staying open to new information and inputs and not allowing our nice, well-tuned mental model to too quickly dismiss or discount new experiences or information. The greatest barrier to being mentally present is often in our own minds. We think we already know the answer, or what works, or why some experience of our own is still superior. We have a great way of editing our reality to suit our intellect. Being mentally present means having the capacity to take in new information without prejudice.

AN ABILITY TO TRUST YOUR GUT

Books such as Malcomb Gladwell's *Blink* have served as a permission slip for leaders to embrace the notion that their visceral instincts should be incorporated into their leadership. Behavioral scientists have yet to pin down exactly where these "guts" reside, but it's a strange brew of primal body chemistry, beliefs, memories and experiences that seem to speak to our rational minds in a language of its own.

A 2011 study published in *Psychological Science* showed how the participants of a card game that had no stated strategy were able to win more often by paying attention to their heart rate and breathing. They had no other data or experience on which to rely other than their "gut instinct." Whether the body was sending signals to the brain or if the body was simply responding to the new signals from the brain, participants performed better when they trusted their guts. This does not obviate the need for clear, rational thought—especially on complex issues—but it does mean that being mentally present involves all of the decision-making capacity we have, even on the thoughts that seem to have a mind of their own.

What unique role does being mentally present play in your success as a leader and in the performance of your team and organization?

We believe leadership thinking can never be reserved to executive management. You want an organization that can "think for itself" so your leadership is scalable. When people see you thinking actively, it can invite them to do the same; they understand thinking about the work—not just doing it—is key to growth and success.

No CEO or executive leader can pretend he or she has all the answers, so fostering a thinking organization invites ideas and innovation on a large scale.

Think about it

Thinking, by its nature, moves the business forward. All great performance comes from doing new things well, and new things are the result of ideas and insights—all of which spring from critical thinking.

The mentally present leader is not just one who gets things done, but one who ignites the human intellect at all levels, starting with his or her own.

You Must be Present to Win. Mentally.

You Must be Present to Win. Mentally.

Chapter 4

Emotionally Present

Put your heart in the right place.

"Get Loud!"

We all see that cheer flashed up on the Jumbotron at football stadiums, but a few years ago during a Kansas City Chiefs game at Arrowhead Stadium, it took on some added importance.

The Chiefs were having a magical season. They started 9 - 0. Every weekend, when the Chiefs were playing at home in Arrowhead Stadium, it was loud. Very loud! So loud that Chiefs management decided that they wanted to set the record and become the loudest outside stadium in the world.

They had their reasons.

Century Link Field in Seattle held the record for the loudest outdoor stadium at that time. It earned the title after Seattle Seahawks running back Marshawn Lynch scampered 67 yards for a touchdown in a 2011 playoff game and the fans exploded in roars so cacophonous as to register on seismic meters nearby.

So in 2013 the goal was to outdo the Seattle crowd, and Kansas City was up for the challenge. Just to keep the feat beyond dispute, the Chiefs hired an official from Guinness World Records to stand on the sidelines during the game to document the effort. It turned out to be Philip Robertson, who had been the same official who had measured the 137 decibel level at the Seattle Seahawks game two seasons earlier.

Stacking The Deck

To ensure fans were riled up enough for this, the Chiefs chose the game against one of their biggest rivals—the Oakland Raiders. A couple of times during the game, the messages scrolled across the stadium Jumbotron instructing the crowd to "Get Loud."

But it didn't work. The Chiefs were going to come up short as the game wound down.

In the fourth quarter, the crowd noise reached 135 decibels, and that's where the fans thought they were going to end up. Many fans dropped their heads in disappointment. Not because the Chiefs were going to lose the game. The Chiefs had a slight lead even though the outcome was still in question. The fans were disappointed because they didn't think they would break the record and become the loudest outdoor stadium in the world... until late in the fourth quarter.

The Raiders defense stopped the Chiefs, got the ball on offense and started to drive the football for a potential game-winning score. The momentum had changed in favor of the Raiders. Raiders quarterback Terrelle Prior threw a pass—a bullet. The Raiders receiver got into position, put his hands up to grab that pass and change the outcome of the game. But instead of the Raiders player catching it, Chiefs cornerback Marcus Cooper jumped in front of him, snatching the ball from the Raiders receiver's outstretched arms, and sealing the win for the still-undefeated Kansas City Chiefs.

The crowd erupted instantaneously and spontaneously. The stadium's press box shook hard. The meter in Philip Robertson's hand said it all—137.5 decibels—the loudest outdoor stadium in the world. Just to put that in context, 137.5 decibels is *louder* than what you would experience standing 50 feet away from a military fighter jet using full afterburners to take off from the deck of an aircraft carrier.

All that noise from people. They couldn't plan it. They couldn't organize it. They couldn't do it on cue. They couldn't do it on command.

There had to be another explanation.

They couldn't plan it, organize it, or do it on cue.

It was about emotional energy. Those fans yelled as loud as they could time after time in that game, but there just seemed to be a natural, physical limit to how loud they could be. The exercise of yelling when instructed to do so was simply an intellectual exercise.

Only when the undefeated season and their pride was on the line did everything change. Fans found a reserve of energy and capacity, because their motivations became emotional. To this day, I'm convinced they had not planned to set that sound record in that moment. They may have even forgotten all about it in the exuberance of that unexpected interception and touchdown. But in that moment, they experienced and achieved a form of greatness they never imagined.

This was no fluke, by the way. In fact, Seattle came right back and beat the Chiefs' sound barrier by a mere tenth of a decibel—137.6 decibels.

Double Down

It looked like that new record was unassailable by the Chiefs, who during the 2014 season were on a four-game losing skid. Next up: The world champion New England Patriots, certainly a drubbing in the making, holding special humiliation given that it was a Monday Night Football game.

When the game started, however, that anxiety fell away. The Chiefs intercepted passes thrown by New England's star quarterback Tom Brady twice and one was returned for a touchdown. Brady was strip-sacked by the Chiefs swarming defense to set up a field goal. Very quickly the Chiefs were leading the world champion Patriots by a score of 17 to 0.

With eight seconds remaining until halftime, at the very moment the timeout was called, up 17 - 0, the fans in Arrowhead Stadium realized the feat their team was accomplishing and got emotional again. The stadium was rocking as the fans realized they were part of something even bigger. Again, the sound measuring devices told the story as much as the scoreboard—142.2 decibels. The fans shattered the old record.

The stadium was rocking.

The Chiefs handed the Patriots their worst loss in 10 years that night, but that was simply the outcome of an emotionally charged environment that gave the team and its fans hope, resolve and confidence.

The first time Chiefs fans set the sound record, it was spontaneous. The second time certainly was driven by emotion, but this time it had a bit of intent mixed in with it. (The stadium had handed out 37,000 earplugs at the gate before the game.) Sure, the hard-luck Chiefs were about to vanquish the world champs before a home crowd, but the fans also had already experienced what they could do with that reserve emotional energy. They were able to summon it again when the circumstances called for it.

The first time, they acted different. The second time, they *became* something different. They trusted and leveraged emotional energy in the moment.

They were emotionally present.

 Too many executives distrust their emotions or the emotions of their followers.

We are taught to do that. In engineering, information technology and math, facts and formulas reign supreme. Almost any problem can be solved through the rational and clinical application of formula and design.

Trust Your Emotions

In finance and business management courses, the breeding grounds for many senior executives and especially CEOs, we are schooled to govern emotion. To temper impulse, trust research, and base decisions in fact and logic is the cultural norm. We have enough ambiguity to manage; we are taught to keep messy emotions out of it.

Facts can usually be filtered and sorted down to a clear reality; emotions ramble across the whole range of human experience and are pretty hard to always understand or corral. At worst, some people think the degree of emotional expression or drive is inversely proportional to intellect—the more we feel, the less we think.

As well, many executives labor under the misunderstanding that leadership is about staying cool, reserved and a bit distant as a well-intended practice to remain independent in their thinking and actions.

It's time to challenge that belief.

Logic or Emotion

We have heard that we make decisions emotionally and rationalize them intellectually. This is why we read the brochures with all of the specifications *after* we have bought the car or the new appliance. Our dens or kitchens or garages are museums to the tenet that we are driven by emotions, not logic, in making decisions.

Emotions are more
powerful than logic.

Research in decision theory and behavioral science gave scant notice to emotions up through most of the 20th century, with social scientists and behavioral psychologists leaning in favor of cognitive theory in explaining how one makes decisions. However, beginning in the 1970s, researchers opened up to the notion that emotions play a powerful role in our choices, even subordinating rational thinking. (So, if people on any given day think they're out of their minds in following you, they may be on to some truth there!)

A Powerful Stew

Before we consider their role in decisions, what do we mean by "emotion?" In simple terms, emotions are non-cognitive sentiments, moods or visceral states that are more felt than thought. Psychologists will tell you these "states" emerge out of murky places—our genes, our early life experiences, our belief structure, our worst fears and our greatest hopes.

A 2014 research summary by behavioral scientists at Harvard, University of California-Riverside and Carnegie Mellon noted that emotions can often be the defining influence in decisions, easily swamping fact. These emotions can arise from the direct circumstances (integral), or be carried over to other unrelated situations (incidental emotions). In other words, we may have an emotional reaction to something we see right in front of us, but those same emotions can often arise under a similar set of circumstances later, even if situations have little parallel.

Emotions inform our intellect. That may be discouraging to higher-minded folks, but it is core to the human experience.

Emotions inform our intellect.

The overwhelming body of research on this shows that emotions can affect how deeply we think, can distort our sense of reality and may filter out unwanted inputs. To understand the interconnection of emotions to any one individual and sort it out into a rational framework is like unraveling steel wool. No wonder facts serve as a refuge.

Break Down Barriers

The good news in all of this is that emotions can also help us overcome the rationality that serves as a barrier. Sometimes the greatest achievements in life are the result of what seemed like a crazy or stupid dream the night before.

Emotions are woven into our deepest desires and our most ambitious dreams. How often have you dutifully listed the pros and cons of a decision on two columns of a paper, only to be disappointed that the cons outnumbered the pros, or how the longer list of pros somehow felt clinical and uninspiring?

Emotions matter greatly in leadership because when we connect with individuals on an emotional level, we are tapping into that deep well in our people—the one that propels them to action and marshals their resolve—because what we want from them has an emotional tie to what they want for themselves. When we connect with them as humans, we set the stage to connect them to our organizational mission.

People don't charge hills or ford streams because of a business plan or strategy. They move to that level because of passionate, connected leaders with a plan and strategy.

Connect to simply means drawing the shortest line between someone's personal goals and the mission of the organization. When people feel the organization is a great place for them to realize or live out what they see as their best talents and ambitions, they do great work.

Connect with simply means the ability to reach someone's heart as well as their mind. We don't pledge our greatest passion to business plans; we assign our greatest energy to people with good business plans. We don't lay in front of trains or jump over waterfalls for business plans, but we will reach pretty deeply and give our all when we feel really connected with a great leader.

Connecting *to* and connecting *with* are central to the action plan of being emotionally present. When we can make the emotional connection between the hopes and ambitions of the company with what people want to experience in their own lives, we are on to something.

That Monday night in Arrowhead Stadium, the Chiefs fans wanted to set the record and become the loudest outdoor stadium in the world. But what they really wanted was to win the game. When Marcus Cooper intercepted the ball and sealed the victory for the undefeated Kansas City Chiefs, he gave them what they really wanted—the victory. Only then was breaking the sound record easy. I once had a boss who did the same thing.

As Chief Operating Officer, my job was to oversee physical operations of the company. My job—at least on the organization chart—was not to be the voice of the company. That role was most often taken by my boss, the CEO.

I loved my work. Put me in a power plant out in the field with my people, in a tough, complicated operations planning meeting, and I felt at home. (I still love to share my stories, teach people, get in front of audiences and just enjoy the energy in that interaction.) My boss Mark figured that out about me. He found a way for me to teach, inspire, lead and grow other leaders in a very public and passionate way, while at the same time advancing the mission of the company. Mark connected what I really wanted to do with the mission of the organization.

Taking a Chance

I remember one particular instance when we were rolling out our company strategy for electric cars. The company had made a significant investment in electric cars and charging stations. We needed to roll out and communicate our plans and strategies to city and state leaders, our customers and the general public. We needed to communicate our mission to everyone, so somebody needed to communicate publicly. Somebody needed to give a speech on the street in front of our corporate headquarters to the invited public leaders, the press and the crowd that was sure to gather.

> He was a great leader because he could connect what I really wanted to do with the greater mission of the organization.

Mark could have picked the logical choice—the corporate public relations spokesperson, or one of the engineers, the experts at electric transportation—but instead, Mark chose me.

Why?

He knew that I strongly believed in the electric car strategy and that I wanted that strategy to succeed. He also knew what I really wanted to do: public speaking. He saw me enjoy public communications, and he also saw my commitment to studying, practicing and constantly working on improving my speaking skills.

Mark is an emotionally present leader. He took the time to know my dreams and what really lit me up, not just what was on my job description. He was also a great leader because he could connect what I really wanted to do with the greater mission of the organization. You might think that he was simply aligning people's skills with what the company needed. You might say that Mark was just being an efficient manager and getting the right people in the right roles. Or as Jim Collins says in his book, *Good to Great*, "the right people in the right seats on the bus." However, it was much bigger than that to me. It meant the world to me.

Connection
shouts
human care and
ownership.

Connection Matters

When leaders figure out what people really want to do and then connect that to the mission of the organization, it shouts human care and ownership. Nothing is more motivating than ownership. What Mark did was one of the most motivating things that ever happened in my career. Whether it was a ribbon cutting for a new building or plant, an employee leadership talk or just a general company announcement, I wanted to get better each time Mark asked me to speak.

The same thing happened in the safety area. Mark knew I had a passion for employee safety. When the company-wide safety tour was scheduled, requiring a huge amount of time away from the office and the other executives on the team, Mark knew I should be there leading that effort and speaking at every meeting. He made sure I was not called on to do anything else except the safety tour.

In fact, whenever public speaking needed to be done, many times Mark selected me for the task. I had a passion for leadership development, so Mark cleared the way for me to speak to all new leaders and gave me a role in most of the company's leadership development workshops. Pretty quickly, I became "in demand" and those holding leadership or safety sessions were calling me directly.

When something is really personally motivating, it just makes you perform at your best and strive to become better. I'd like to suggest that while I grew and benefitted from that motivation, so too did the company as it also got what it needed.

That is a win-win!

Our work together over the years, which led to this book, reflects a deep belief in emotional presence and the powerful sense of purpose that comes from that.

People don't slay dragons without a profound sense of purpose. When people hear their leader talk about what they do and why they do it, they must see and feel the emotion. It's more than body language or tone; it's that subtle but profound sense that we are rallying a common bond as fellow human beings.

You can tag whatever words you want to that—passion, conquering fear, experiencing transforming change, care, courage, humility—and you come up with lists of human emotions.

People don't slay dragons without a profound sense of purpose.

Being emotionally present doesn't mean wearing your emotions on your sleeve. Raw emotional expression has its place, but no one will follow someone for very long who cries a lot, admits too easily to fear, or even cares a bit too much.

Emotional presence is grounded in a belief that emotions are what connect us as human beings. Emotions unleash some powerful chemistry inside of us to help us overcome barriers to realize something we truly want.

Leaders Don't Scroll

A leader is not a Jumbotron. A leader is so much more.

The Kansas City Chiefs tried to tell the fans when to get loud by scrolling the message across the stadium screen. That message didn't do anything. Simply telling people what to do doesn't work. You can't just hold a big meeting, read a nice speech, tell them the mission or announce the change you want to see and expect them to get it. It takes more than that.

Leaders must show others their commitment. We must connect with people on a human level. Be real; be a human being. All human beings care about something. We are naturally passionate beings. When we connect with our people, we are tapping into that and highlighting a commonality between us.

When we connect passion to our organization's mission and purpose, we are leveraging it for a greater good.

Emotional presence should be part of your leadership platform.

One of the most effective ways to incorporate emotional presence is to develop an "emotional statement."

This is your personal testimony that tells others that you are "all in."

Everybody needs to have their own emotional statement.

I also have applied this notion of "connect to" in my work as a senior executive of utility company operations.

On the surface, someone might question what's so inspirational or world-changing about keeping the lights on? Not me! I believe electricity is life-giving! Think about life without electricity. Without access to reliable and affordable electricity, life is not the same. Without access to electricity, the infant mortality rates are double, the life span is much shorter, and the quality of life is lower on nearly every scale. In fact, for us in the developed world, we can't function without electricity. Now think about how lucky I was to be able to provide electricity to people for most of my life! Electricity is life-giving. Electricity is like freedom. You cannot lead something that you are not deeply passionate about.

You can't lead something that you are not passionate about.

You can tell we care about this. We want you to feel our emotional energy. Hang around either of us for very long and you'll get a really good idea of what we care about. And if we care about the right things—the same things you do—now we can move ahead together in ways no business plan or speech or coaching method can ever do alone.

Master Your Emotions

Being emotionally present means, of course, that you have to be comfortable in your own skin. Emotions don't have a mind of their own; they arise from your own experience, beliefs, values and—yes—triggers. Don't be afraid of them, master them. Respect that emotions are important to help you connect with people on a whole different level.

It has often been said in the public speaking field that people will remember how you made them feel much longer than what you said. The same is true for leadership when you master emotional energy.

People perform better when they do what they care about most, and emotions are the signals that tell you where those cares reside.

You Must be Present to Win. Emotionally.

Chapter 5

The Price of
the Ticket

**There's no such thing
as a free raffle.**

Take a deep breath.

If you've reached this far in the book, you probably have bought into the notion of being physically, mentally and emotionally present, and feel you are ready to learn how to make that a regular part of your leadership.

Now is the time for you to step back and take into consideration what this will require of you because if you don't, you likely will falter or fade from the commitment.

Everything worthwhile in our lives comes at a cost—either now or later. Cost is only an obstacle when it asks more of us than the reward. That seems simple enough, but in the case of your leadership presence, we want to challenge you in a big way about what it will take.

You will need to be "all-in."

People can sniff out pretense pretty easily. If being present as we have proposed is simply something you do when you are comfortable, when it feels good, when it is convenient or when it gives you some jollies, it will not work.

Early in my career, I figured out that the people who got ahead were those who dressed well. In particular, they dressed "up" for the job they wanted. Look good, get ahead. A simple formula.

So, sporting a nice, pressed white shirt and a carefully selected tie, I stepped off the elevator, brimming with confidence and ambition. For most in the room, this was just a typical meet-and-greet gathering, but not for me. This was my chance to create a great first impression and, honestly, to prove that I was worthy to be included in this select group of leaders.

My Ink Spot

As the elevator doors opened, the light and clamor from the room hit me in the face. I looked down at the floor as I walked out of the elevator, and that's when I saw it: A huge, black ink spot on my new white dress shirt.

It started at the bottom of the pocket and trailed a couple of inches out in all directions onto the shirt. It was big, wet and oozing.

I panicked.

This business meeting that I was walking into was important, not only because of the topics being addressed, but also because of who would be in the room. My thoughts immediately went back to the hand-written note from the CEO appointing me to this committee and the invitation attached to it. I was going to be in impressive company; also on the invitation were listed the mayor, the city manager, the head of economic development, a college president (who also served on our company's board), and a couple of big company CEOs. I knew those people would all be judging me, wondering what qualified me to be serving on this important committee and attending this meeting. You see, I was only in my mid-30s and had just been promoted to vice president. My company's CEO hand-picked me to be the organization's single member on this important civic committee. He trusted me to make a great first impression.

That's when I saw it: A huge, black ink spot on my new white dress shirt.

Well, I was about to make a memorable first impression all right!

Apparently, while on my way to the meeting, my pen had leaked. I don't know how it happened, but it happened. Black ink found my white shirt like chewed gum finds the soles of your shoes. Now I know why those engineers who always carry an army of writing tools use pocket protectors.

At first I tried to avoid the embarrassment by escaping. I immediately turned around to go back into the elevator, but the doors banged shut in my face. There was no alternate escape route in sight. I started talking to myself, maybe out loud, I don't remember. "What can I do? Think man, think! You can't just stand here facing the elevator forever!"

So I turned around, using my hand as a shield to hide my ink spot, while I looked for another way out and bought some time.

Then I saw it—the registration table. That was it. That was my way out!

Everybody knows what you pick up from the registration table before meetings where lots of people don't know each other's names. Sure, a nametag. And where do you think my nametag went?

In Olympic record time, I located the nametag containing my name, quickly peeled off the slick back cover and slapped it directly over the ink spot. Bam! Problem solved! I thought I was golden!

I went on in and joined the other attendees, gliding swiftly and confidently into mingle mode.

Not so fast.

About 30 minutes had passed when Grady, a middle-aged, well dressed, distinguished-looking man came up to me, glanced at my name tag and said, "Doug, nice to meet you."

"Nice to meet you, too," I replied as I shook his hand and looked him directly in his eyes so as to guide his view up to my face and away from the area around my nametag.

He immediately leaned in toward me and whispered, "Hey Doug, I can see your ink spot."

Now I did not know this man at the time, but Grady's soft voice stopped me in my tracks. Grady's words made me realize how foolish I really was. Anybody who looked at my nametag would notice the ink spot—and they all were looking at my nametag since I was a first timer. I wasn't fooling anybody.

Cover our Flaws

That day I had a flaw that I did not want anybody to see. I was embarrassed because I was not perfect.

"Hey Doug, I can see your ink spot."

Do you think that Grady was the only one who saw that ink spot? I spent 30 minutes mingling in the crowd.

How many other people do you think saw the ink spot but just didn't bother to confront me? Maybe it felt awkward to note my flaw. Maybe they didn't want to embarrass me. Or, worse, maybe they walked away chuckling to themselves about how foolish I really looked.

We desperately want to believe that we can actually get away with hiding our imperfections. We hang on to the belief that we are fooling people by concealing our weaknesses and flaws. Making a great first impression has always been important to me. My greatest fear is that I will do something stupid and make a bad impression. At that moment, when I was caught in a situation of doubt and weakness, I concealed what seemed to be a trivial thing, and made it take on much greater proportion.

Nice Job, Doug.

Can we really fool people by attempting to hide our flaws? And can we really pretend that we can hide them all? All leaders have weaknesses, faults and ink spots of their own. My coach, Paul, always told me that he never found a flaw in a leader that the followers didn't already know about. We all see the flaws and the ink spots in others, but people still think their spots are well-hidden.

You can be an effective leader in spite of your flaws. So many books written by leadership experts attempt to fix your flaws. They promise that once we are free of these nasty ink spots, we can lead effectively.

It's just not true.

I don't know what your flaws, doubts and fears are, but if you're human, I know you've got them.

The fact is that leaders must lead effectively despite our imperfections.

Vulnerability is NOT easy.

The notion of baring something of ourselves before others is enough to make our skin crawl.

There's a good reason for that.

In our lives, particularly in our business lives, we get pretty proficient at building up veneers. These veneers are practiced behaviors and ways of speaking to show the image of ourselves we want to project to others. They are, by training, outside-in, meaning much of what we project to the world is designed to conform or appeal to those we want to attract or impress.

Let's stipulate right now that this is not entirely wrong. In fact, in its best forms, it can convey a message of respect to others that we care about coming across as confident, poised, polished or whatever attributes you feel are measured by others. It informs our choice of words, our selection of attire, the tenor of our voice, our mannerisms, and just about everything we associate with creating an impression.

It can also, however, be a shield.

We get pretty proficient at
building up veneers —
practiced behaviors to show the
image of ourselves we want to
project to others.

A long-standing study by Gallup shows a remarkable contrast between what senior executives think are essential to
their role of leading others and what those people say they
need from their leader. Ranked high on the list by executives were qualities like creativity, global awareness, innovation and business acumen. Hard to argue those are not
among the currencies of great leaders. However, ask the
people they lead, and they came up with a notably different list: honesty, integrity, courage and openness.

Why the disconnect?

I believe a lot of it can be traced to formal business edu-
cation. Can you imagine a top-tier business school
offering classes on honesty, approachability or courage?
Of course not; those business classes on strategy, financial management and business analysis have harder
edges to them. They are way more comfortable areas to
explore, and more easily measured.

What those hard-edged business classes do is teach you
what to do, and certainly some teach *how* to do it. Most
of the leadership attributes ranked highly by executives

are about what they do. On the employee list, though, is *who* they are.

In my experience coaching more than 150 clients over 20 years, the inescapable fact is that no matter our station in life, no matter how superior our intellect, no matter how unrivaled our track record of success, we are the product of our story. We all have hopes and dreams and fears and anxieties.

We are the product of our story.

Doubts and Fears

When we face situations of doubt and fear and lack genuine confidence in who we are, we can act against everything we stand for.

This fact is easy to dismiss, but ask yourself:

- → Do I only choose to involve myself in situations where I feel confident?

- → Do I prefer working on projects instead of with people?

- → Do I push blame up (or down) the ladder?

- → If someone asks me an honest question, is my first instinct to give an honest answer or hold back?

- → How do I feel about my last big failure, and does anyone know how I feel?

In working at being present, it's essential to understand ourselves and confront some of these barriers because people will sense when we are holding back or just acting out practiced mannerisms. What matters is not to act OUT OF FEAR but to act THROUGH OUR FEARS. If you are fearless, you are not human.

Vulnerability.

We hear it a lot, but how do we feel about that word?

In my work with senior executive clients, one of the key thresholds is when they approach that point of vulnerability. How they act in that moment is key to whether they will grow or fall back behind the façade.

What matters is not to act OUT OF FEAR but to act THROUGH OUR FEARS.

If you are in a position of authority—or simply in a role where people count on you—vulnerability can seem counter-productive if not destructive. And to be sure, it can be both of those things when not exercised in the appropriate way and to the right measure.

However, vulnerability can have a powerful influence in developing the depth of relationships and trust we have talked about in this book.

By instinct, we want to follow people of courage and conviction. That sense of bravery and clarity they project can overcome our own fears and doubts. It is what one of my CEO clients calls "positive faith"—a fierce discipline that drives you to do the right things in the right way even when the actual outcome is unknown. Staying at it as a habit eventually brings the right outcomes into focus and increases your odds of reaching them. Dithering in doubt does not. Courage is not the absence of fear but the will to move ahead amid your fears.

So, how does vulnerability fit into that, and why does it matter?

While leadership courage can get you through the tough times, it can wear thin if that's the only card we show. The people who follow you are often painfully aware of their own faults and frailties; when they never see the same in you, it can leave them feeling lessened. On the other end of the spectrum, they may eventually see you as disingenuous, as if your courage is a practiced art rather than a true, tested quality.

Courage can get you through the tough times, but it can wear thin if that's the only card we show.

Vulnerability is not a psyche-unzipping, soul-baring, emotionally wrought display of weakness; it is simply the humble, honest and open acknowledgement of our humanness. As leaders, when we become vulnerable, we become approachable, accessible and, ultimately, believable.

Vulnerability levels us. It says no matter our station in life, we have a commonality among us as people. Our hopes, dreams, fears and ambitions for our lives are often more universal than we know. But life, as we all know, does not come as a perfect picture. We have flaws, faults, blind spots and even painful stories that are all part of the puzzle of who we are. When we put down the façade and discard the pretense, we become more real to those we lead.

Authenticity

We have heard for years now about the importance of being an authentic leader. Authenticity means that your actions match your words, your behaviors represent a natural extension of your values and not some rehearsed manner. *The only path to authenticity is through vulnerability.*

In Doug's story, he suffered that moment of exposure and took it with grace—eventually! His vulnerability (admittedly only after his secret was out) allowed others to relate to him because of their own failures. He allowed them to step into his moment of vulnerability and help.

That's one of the often-overlooked bonuses of vulnerability; it does not just serve the needs of others, it serves us. When we are vulnerable, we realize we are not alone.

Being vulnerable when being present is to make the most of that experience. You'll probably find it's quite natural once you realize how good you have become at avoiding it! It may take the form of the good self-effacing comment, perhaps a bit of our own story, even a humble acceptance of a failure, but vulnerability brings freshness and a credibility to our efforts to be present.

Being present demands that we be vulnerable. Being present means being in close quarters—on the spot, on the job, in the moment—and it's a fool's errand to think we can pretend to be something we are not. People can see through pretense; they can sense the distance.

The ending to my ink spot debacle points out another benefit of vulnerability.

After Grady was courageous enough to warn me of my ridiculous plight, he offered, "Hey Doug, I can see that is new, white dress shirt. If you will bring that shirt to my car after this meeting, I will take it by my dry cleaning shop tonight and will get it back to you in the morning."

Cleaning the Spot

I was uncomfortable handing over my dress shirt and leaving in my T shirt, but I took Grady's offer. Sure enough. The next morning my crisp, white dress shirt was hanging in a clear plastic dry cleaner bag—ink spot gone!

Grady saved my shirt, but he did much more for me. I learned that through being vulnerable, I allowed somebody else to shine. My vulnerability actually helped somebody else and me in the process.

Doug's metaphor for the principles in this book is that every raffle has tickets.

Each one of those tickets holds a potential of reward—not a guarantee, just a potential. It is only worth something when it is selected, turned in and redeemed for something of real value.

As leaders, your organizational position offers a ticket. It is not worth much to you or others unless you understand the potential it carries. The potential is the talent, passion, mindfulness and presence you bring to your role as a leader.

Go All In

When we are called, we turn in that ticket. We go "all in" regarding what we offer to our people. That ticket is not free. It will cost you convenience, energy to get to know your people and time investing in their stories, while being open about your own.

Leadership is not a role; it is a calling.

Have your ticket ready.

Leadership is not a role; it is a calling.

Chapter 6

What's Your Ticket Worth?

More than the cost of the paper it's printed on.

Everybody has a ticket.

One day, at some point in the future, you or your company will face a big challenge. You may be facing that challenge right now. It may be something that you have never experienced before, and it probably has leadership written all over it. It will be just like the raffle. Somehow, your name will be the one on the ticket.

Your name will be called.

In the raffle, when a name is called and nobody answers, who loses? Sure, the person whose name is on the ticket loses. But really, we all lose. We don't get to celebrate with a winner. The same is true with leadership. When you are not present when your name is called, you lose and so does everybody else.

Leaders who are present win.

But more importantly, the people they lead also win.

Leaders Must Be Present To Win®.

On the day of the car raffle, 6,000 people had written their names on little blue tickets, but only a thousand people showed up for the drawing. Leadership is just like that. Many people apply. Many people want to be a leader. Few really show up.

What are you going to do with your ticket? Where will you be when they call your name?

Are you where the action is? Are you physically present?

Are you in tune with your people, the operations and the inner workings of your business? Are you mentally present?

Are you connecting with people on a human level and connecting them to the mission? Are you emotionally present?

What are you going to do with your ticket?

We challenge you to take what you have learned from this book and be "Present to Win" physically, mentally, and emotionally.

It's time to act.

Chapter 7

The Action Plan

Success begins with a plan.

Leadership requires action.

Why do we need an action plan?

Coming from me as a leadership coach, that seems like a ridiculous question, but it is crucial to whether you are to become a "present" leader.

The concepts of Must Be Present To Win, while perhaps new in terms of how they are presented in this book, are really nothing new. We can fairly easily assign intellectual assent to the notion that we have to be in touch with our business and its people, be actively thinking about what to do next or better, and to be invested emotionally in the effort.

If it's that apparent, why aren't we doing it?

We make the mistake of underestimating how fundamental this change in leadership behavior is to many. Doug, in many ways, was a natural for these precepts, but he would tell you that there were times in his career when he had to make changes—sometimes deeply personal in terms of what he valued within himself—to become the present leader he seeks to be.

I've seen it often in my coaching practice. We mean well, but good intentions can fade in the press of the urgent or when externalities bear down on us.

I'm going to assume that you are reading this book because you want to learn how to be a present leader. Maybe you already do some of what we have talked about but want to get better at it. Maybe you hadn't ever considered the ideas presented in this book. No matter where you are on this leadership continuum, if you truly desire to become a more present leader, you must be willing to make a change. This philosophy is not just something else to add to your repertoire as an executive leader. It needs to be central to your thinking and behaviors in order to have the maximum effect on you and others. As such, it must summon within you the will to change, perhaps in a big way.

> ## If you truly desire to become a more present leader, you must be willing to make a change.

I seek to connect my clients' desires to change with something they truly want in their lives. When clients come to me with lists of coaching goals that someone else says they need to address, I tell them that we're not likely to get far until they come back with a list of things that they want for themselves. It may be the same list, but if it's not connected with something the clients want for themselves, the goals won't last. When my clients get to the point where they really want something for their lives—business or personal—we start to see transformational change.

Transformational change does not come when someone else says you need it; it comes when you want it deeply.

Being a Present Leader is Difficult

Being a present leader will be inconvenient. It is not a safe place to abide. It will require you to change your daily routines, your disciplines, perhaps even how you measure you sense of value. A fully present leader is a transformational leader. Status quo may have been your obstacle; it is now your enemy.

Personal change is hard because we have to strip the circuitry built up over many years of experience, practice and beliefs. Our brains are designed to learn, adapt and take in new experiences. Yes, that same brain wants very much to get things compartmentalized and organized into predictable sets to identify patterns and follow them. Change—unless imposed on us from external threats or opportunities—is actually not a natural state of the human condition. We have to disrupt that.

The likelihood of change is greatly increased when the following three conditions are present:

→ A profound dissatisfaction with the status quo;

→ A clear vision of a future state; and

→ Small, achievable steps that give you a sense of progress and momentum.

That's it. Simple.

Except, each step is an undertaking in and of itself and can't be skipped.

Be Very Unhappy with Now

Being profoundly dissatisfied with the status quo means you have to be restlessly discontent with how well you lead, with how physically, mentally and emotionally present you are in your enterprise. If you're not, you will always have a comfortable place to retreat to when it gets hard or inconvenient. This is the "push" that drives you out of where you are today.

Status quo may have been your obstacle; it is now your enemy.

What makes you profoundly dissatisfied is up to you, but get there. Maybe it's a 360° assessment that points out your gaps. Maybe a talk with a trusted aide who can tell you the truth. Maybe the best truth-teller is your calendar. Is it full of meetings, outside appointments, civic/business gatherings or direct reports tromping to your office with project updates? Maybe it is a self-assessment. Do a quick check of the heartbeat of your day. Do you go from one urgency to the next with barely enough time to take a breath? How is that working out for you? Really?

You get the idea. Where is the intentional think time? Where are the scheduled and committed times out of the office visiting operating sites or customers? Where we spend our time (and money) is the only reliable measure of our priorities. St. Catherine of Siena, a 14th century nun devoted to serving the poor, had it right when she said, "You become like what you serve." If we want to be someone who connects well with people and is understood and trusted, we have to exercise the daily routines that put us in the places where those skills and qualities become natural.

Do people often misjudge your motives? Would they say your emotions are a strength or weakness? If you hedge these answers, or convince yourself you're actually doing pretty well, you likely will not get markedly better at it. That's just a fact of human nature and change. If you're willing to get a little disgusted at yourself in this area—maybe call it laziness or distraction—you're at least a third of the way toward the changes Doug and I are championing.

You become like what you serve.

All of these inputs or influences into whether you are intolerant of your status quo are "pushes"—forces that bear down on your mindset and attitudes. Simply put, it is pressure. Pressure is good sometimes, but it is not sustainable, either because its source ebbs in energy (your friends give up trying to tell you something), or you become conditioned to or resilient against these pressures. Pressure—or push—can initiate action but can rarely sustain it.

Your Future Self

Having a clear vision of the future state is the "pull." Your employees, likely have a view of what they would like you to be as a leader. This is your chance to step up to that. Think about people you admire or who have been instrumental in your development as a leader, and invariably you will find someone who was "present" in the ways we've outlined. In my experience, a good image of your future self will keep tugging on you to stay with this change.

Small Steps

Finally, what is the role of these small, achievable steps that give you a sense of progress and momentum? The small steps part is a bit contrary to what you often hear. Others will tell you to take that big leap, go big or go home. Certainly, there is a time and a place to commit in a grand expression, to experience some abandon, the visceral shudder of immersing yourself in an entirely new and inescapable experience.

However, when it comes to a sustained change—one that is fully integrated into who you are as a leader—small steps win out. We are talking about new habits, new routines and new rhythms. We are talking about the long game here, not just a thrill. The small steps work with our brain wiring, reprogramming our neural pathways. Just like developing mastery of a craft, it takes time, repetition and practice. Small steps offer you the juice that comes with a sense of accomplishment. Our action plan is designed to feed this sense of progress and success. This is not a crash diet plan to new leadership. This approach is a steady, disciplined, intentional action that builds habits and rhythms.

Steady, disciplined, intentional action builds habits and rhythms.

In my experience, people often struggle with the vision of what and who comes out of this change. For people gifted with a boss or a role model who reflected these areas of leadership presence, the vision is clearer. Doug was given such a gift early in his career.

Pay your dues.

We've all heard that phrase at some point early in our careers. While I retired as a C-level executive, the path to that position had some humble beginnings.

And some of my greatest learning.

My journey started 30 years ago, during my last semester of college. I took a trip to an electric utility to interview for a job. The first time I stepped onto the turbine deck of that power plant I knew that's where I wanted to work and spend my career. I fell in love with that power plant: the hum of the turbines, the aromas of machine oil and the air pierced with the heat of the burners. The sheer scale of everything around me was intoxicating. I went back to my classes with a renewed resolve to finish with my engineering degree and get a job with that electric company.

A few months later, there I was, proud to be making a living 600 miles away from my home, on my own, drawing a paycheck. It was a great thing.

I remember the first time I met him. He always wanted to personally welcome the new employees. Everybody remembers the first time they met Ed Platt. He was a large, imposing, intimidating man. He owned the room. Everybody admired and respected him, but I must admit, I was a little afraid of him.

I remember the first time I met him. Everybody remembers the first time they met Ed Platt.

It didn't take me long to learn some of the culture at that plant, captured in expressions that I would often hear among the workers or maybe see tacked up to a bulletin board. They came from Ed's unique sayings, and everybody knew what they were. They were his principles, his leadership beliefs.

He called them Platt-itudes.

Platt-itude –
Fear is a Healthy Emotion

Ed Platt believed that there needed to be a little tension in the workplace. Not too much—just enough to help us perform at our best. Ed didn't lead with fear, but it played a role even so. The fear didn't come from him; it came from within ourselves. There was just something about that man. You just were afraid to let him down.

One of the practices of this company at that time was to create side agreements to the union contract. Every time management and union labor couldn't find a way to abide by something in the contract, they just created a side agreement. Years and years of side agreements had accumulated. We had so many side agreements, it was hard to rummage through all that clutter to get a clear view of what the labor contract said. Management could not manage the workforce effectively because they couldn't rely on the contract itself as a result of those side agreements. Every time a supervisor tried to take what they thought was an action supported by the contract, a worker would whip out some side agreement from months or years ago and challenge it. It was impossible to keep up. The union reps often stumbled into the same tangle, trying to enforce a rule that had been undermined by yet another side agreement.

Needless to say, it was a mess.

Ed Platt did not like messes, so naturally the side agreements were bound to be the focus of his ire.

There was just something about that man. You just were afraid to let him down.

After long negotiations, he finally executed a contract minus all of those side agreements. They were either negotiated into the contract, becoming part of the labor agreement, or they were negotiated out and no longer existed.

The Big Green Meeting

As soon as the union and management signed the new labor agreement, Ed called an after-hours supervisors meeting. I'll never forget it. It was held in the only building on-site big enough to hold all the supervisors and managers—a big, green, metal maintenance building with a concrete floor and a high ceiling. The room had been cleaned up, with all the equipment cleared out in preparation for this meeting. I remember having never seen it so clean. It was totally bare—except in the center of the room, Ed had placed a 55-gallon drum with a small table beside it.

As everyone shuffled and murmured about, wondering what all this spectacle was for, Ed silently strode into the room with a pile of papers tucked underneath his left arm. He walked up to that barrel in the center of the room without saying a word. Then he placed those papers on that table, pulled out his lighter, and one by one set each sheet of paper on fire, dropping them into the barrel right there for us all to see.

The room was silent, except for the sound of side agreements crackling in that glowing drum.

When he finished burning all of those side agreements, he turned and faced everyone in the room and said, "We have one contract. It's a fair contract. Everybody's agreed upon it. We're going to manage to that contract. Nothing more, nothing less."

Then he picked up that last sheet of paper off the table, held it high and announced, "This is the new side agreement form. If you need to make a new side agreement, fill the front side out completely. When you get done, just flip it over and sign your letter of resignation on the back." He laid that form on the table, slowly scanned the room and quietly walked out the same door he had come in.

We all got the message about side agreements.

How? Ed was quite obviously physically present. He could have sent a letter or forged a new policy on side agreements and posted it to the bulletin board. Nope. He used his personal physical presence to make a point, but also showed a powerful use of emotional presence. It was a calculated, measured determination bordering on disgust or anger. There was no doubt in our minds that it mattered to him, and consequently, needed to matter to us.

Platt-itude – All Accidents and Injuries are Preventable

You hear a lot of companies taking up the mantra about "zero safety incidents" but to say that mantra decades ago in a much more rough-and-tumble manufacturing world was pretty provocative (and likely to elicit some chuckles and scoffs).

Ed declared it back then like it was just as much an unassailable truth as the sun coming up at dawn. "All accidents and injuries are preventable." He was the first guy I ever heard say it. I heard the muttering and saw the eyes rolling among the supervisors, so I was caught between who to believe. Ed was about to make that choice a lot easier, or at least a lot clearer.

"All accidents and injuries are preventable."

Coal-fired power plants get shut down on a scheduled basis to do maintenance. During one such outage, some mechanics were taking apart a coal pipe and were separating a couple of flanges. Some unburned coal fell on the ground and ignited. It started the two mechanics on fire and burned them horribly.

Within minutes, the two injured workers were carted off to a company ambulance in the parking lot and rushed to the hospital. Ed peeled out of the parking lot in his big, white company car and tailgated that ambulance all the way to the hospital. He stayed at the hospital that entire day, through the night and through the next day. He was there doing everything he could for the victims, his men and their families.

When his hospital vigil was over, rather than going home and catching up on sleep, Ed steered that big, white company car right back to the plant.

Another Meeting – Not So Green

We were all summoned to that same green metal main-tenance building with the concrete floor and the high ceiling. I remember walking in thinking, "What the heck am I doing here?" The other engineers and super-visors were thinking and saying the same thing, "That accident didn't happen here in operations, it was over in maintenance. Why are we here? It didn't happen on my watch."

After we all were gathered, Ed nearly blew the hinges off the door coming into that room. He marched to the center of the room and turned to glare at us. I remember Ed's thundering voice echoing off the sheet metal walls. I had never seen anybody so disappointed and angry in a business setting before or since that day. It only took Ed a couple of seconds to convince everybody in the room that this accident was the result of a leadership problem, a management breakdown, and we were all at fault for those men being in the hospital.

Ed nearly blew the hinges off the door coming into that room.

I remember going home that night trying to explain to my young wife what had happened that day at the plant. I had planned to argue that I had no role in that accident, but somehow that never came out.

Emotions are powerful forces. Misused, they can cripple

trust and shut down engagement. Ed Platt was a stern, forceful man, but he kept his emotional energy in check until it was needed. He used it to make a great impact. Ed could have called a meeting and gone over safety statistics and accident analysis reports, but that would not have changed our hearts and minds. His mission that day was not an intellectual exercise; it was to ring the bell of every manager in that group about the responsibilities of leadership.

Our ears rang for a long time after that.

Platt-itude — Numbers Tell a Story

Early on in my time with Ed, he assigned me a task: Put together a binder full of charts, spreadsheets and graphs showing the operating performance of the plant. Frankly, as a cocky young engineer who liked to get out on the plant floor and mix it up with the workers or just walk around and feel close to all that magnificent machinery, this assignment felt like punishment. I felt sentenced to a dreary life as a back-office bookkeeper. What did that task have to do with leading people and having an impact?

Later, I heard from the managers how Ed would flop that binder open at his regular management meetings, trailing his fingers down the tracks of those charts, sometimes holding one up as if scrutinizing a fake $20 bill.

Then the questions would start—not interrogations, but challenges. "Can we do better? Why did this happen? Is there a connection between this or that? What are we missing here?" In planning sessions, Ed sometimes would pop up with an idea or flip some conventional wisdom on its ear and we would be thinking, "Wow, I never thought of that or saw it that way."

In a power plant, a lot of practical influences on your thinking can lead you to value routine and process—as it should be—given that we are dealing with potentially hazardous operations, and equipment that is larger than most four-star hotels. Still, Ed used his intellect to sharpen our thinking, find ways to innovate and prod us to use our critical thinking skills to run a better operation.

Certainly Ed's physical and emotional presence was hard to miss, but I came to respect and admire that his head was also very much in the game. He was mentally present.

Why Role Models Matter

Those are the stories, but what was the lasting impact? There was a payoff, not only for Ed, but also for me and others that made all that effort worthwhile.

As a way to encourage you to take on this action plan with hope and resolve, let me share two incidents that trace right back to my days with Ed to illustrate the impact you can have on your enterprise and others.

Back then I was not the fearless, hard driving leader that Ed was. I didn't adopt his leadership, his Platt-itudes and his influence right away. I was immature enough to believe that I could figure it all out myself. I transferred from that power plant to another. I went from one job to the next and eventually left that company. Over time, the memory of Ed Platt faded from my mind.

> # I was immature enough to believe that I could figure it all out myself.

Until one day, after joining Westar Energy and moving up to the vice president role, I was standing in front of a group of employees at one of our power plants, in a big metal building with a concrete floor and a high ceiling. We were having a heated debate about the importance of safety.

Crossing Over the Line

After hearing enough of all the chatter and arguments, I just blurted out: "I will never trade your health and well-being for getting the lights on or generating electricity."

I didn't plan those words in any offsite executive strategy meeting. I didn't write them out for a speech. It wasn't anything anybody had ever said before.

As I have reflected on that moment over the years, I have come to realize that it came from deep within—from Ed's influence all those years ago.

There was a truth and clarity about that statement that just cut through all the rancor and doubts. Perhaps I had been staying back from the line—as imaginary as it may have been—that said "don't go all in."

That day I crossed that line.

That day
I crossed the line
and there was no
going back.

I showed my passion in a very real way and I knew there wasn't any going back. When somebody in my position makes a bold statement like that, everybody holds you accountable to those words. I figured the plant employees would remember those words I said that day. However, they did something more than that. A few weeks later, I came back to that power plant for another site visit and noticed a new sign on the plant road leading down to the parking lot. You couldn't miss it. On that large sign were my words:

"I will never trade your health and well-being for getting the lights on or generating electricity."

And below it, my signature.

It was right there for everybody to see, including me. That statement triggered a range of improvements—in morale, in operational effectiveness, and notably, in safety. The impact was measurable, meaningful and long-standing.

Making that statement, while not planned, was not ill-considered. I made it personally—physically—in front of the very people who cared about it the most. I made it with obvious conviction and passion, allowing my emotional energy to have impact. And certainly, as the senior executive, I understood we were going to have to apply some fresh thinking to the enormous task of honoring that pledge.

I had a lot more to learn about being a fully-present leader in the years ahead, but that event stands high in my mind as the time when I first really understood the transformative impact of the fully-present leader.

The Best Meeting

The other incident is deeply personal to me, but I think it is part of why this philosophy of presence means so much to me.

On my last business trip before I retired, I traveled to Dallas, Texas. I went there to visit an old friend. It had been 18 years since I had last seen him, so I called in advance to make sure he'd be around and had time to see me. He said he would meet me in his 11th floor elevator lobby.

I remember the elevator doors sliding open, and there he was. His hand was shaking on a cane. He was no longer the intimidating figure of the man from my memories. Even though he didn't own the room, I was still a little afraid.

Ed Platt could still do that to you.

> He may not own the room anymore, but I was still a little afraid.

We had a great conversation. We talked about all the old times, his famous Platitudes, even a few new ones he had coined since my departure.

Before I left that day, Ed gave me a gift. As soon as he handed it to me, a flood of memories overtook me. It was worn, its pages yellowed and dog-eared, but it was the very book that I had been assigned to put together for him all those years ago. I didn't open it because I wanted to spend my last minutes with him just enjoying talking with this old salt of a manager, not staring at pages in a book. But on the plane ride home, I pried it open and started flipping through its pages.

It was as if I was reliving the whole time with Ed years ago. Some handwritten pages contained his Plattitudes. I wondered if he was simply recording them for posterity or if I was seeing in his writing the very creation of those ideas. Other pages showed charts of operating performance and safety improvements, many of them hitting or exceeding goals at the time we thought were a fantasy.

Moreover, I realized that even though Ed's binder had been tucked away all these years, his lessons were very much alive in my career and in the careers of others. There are many of us who were better leaders because of the lessons Ed instilled in us—not in a binder, but by being present physically, mentally and emotionally in our work, day in and day out.

Before I left that day,
Ed gave me a gift.

Ed gave me and many others that ticket to lead.

I can only hope that through my career I have shared that ticket and redeemed what I was given so others can win.

I'm ready to go to work. Are you?

Now we all have that gift; it's the gift of being present.

Chapter 8

Physically Present Action Plan

If it's worth it – it's worth scheduling.

Imagine a future state where you are out there, physically present with the people you need to see, going places you need to go, visiting with people you need to engage and letting them show you the work they do. You are on your feet, accessible and visible, communicating and gaining trust. That's what we all want. So how do we get there?

The answer is simple. In fact, it is the same method you already use when you really want to get something done, be somewhere at a specific time or meet an important commitment.

You schedule it!

We know the questions already forming in your head. Do I really need to schedule something as simple as being physically present? Doesn't that happen naturally? Don't I already get out of the office every once in a while?

But do you?

We all plan to be physically present at some time in the near future (because in the future we are all wonderful people). In the future, we always call our mothers, we eat less, we exercise more and we generously give our time to others. And we always make time to be physically present.

In the future, we are all wonderful people.

But the future isn't reality. For example, at bedtime you plan (in the future) to get out of bed at 6 a.m. and go to that exercise class you've been avoiding. When you look at your future, you are the kind of person who springs to life early in the morning and actually enjoys exercise. However, in reality, when 6 a.m. arrives, you are no longer that health-serious person because it is now the present, and the present you stays in bed drinking coffee until 8 a.m., planning again to go to that exercise class tomorrow, in the future.

At the start of our day or week, we plan (in the future) to get out of our office and go see people, visit with people, and get a feel for the pulse of our organization. In the future, we are a physically present leader. Once the day starts, the paperwork, meetings, email, phone calls and everyday crises fill our time. Being physically present gets put off yet another day or week because we are too busy to make it happen. We have great intentions. However, we are judged on our actions, not our intentions.

We all have great intentions,
but the paperwork, meetings,
email, phone calls and
everyday crises fill our time,
so we put it off.

We live in the present, but we plan for the future. If we are really going to commit to being physically present, we must plan it and schedule it.

I bet you find it easy to think about the future and make commitments. That's how we are built.

Behavioral economists have shown that making good choices is easy if you don't have to fulfill them now. For example: If you ask me to place a lunch order for next week, I'm likely to pick healthier choices than if I'm drooling over the buffet I'll eat now. The phenomenon is referred to as hyperbolic discounting—the tendency to overvalue rewards now and undervalue them later.

Why is this important when it comes to scheduling time to be physically present? This cognitive bias works in your favor when you are committing to being physically present in the future. Since you don't see the pain right away, it will be easier to commit your time in the future.

So, looking ahead at open space on your calendar, you are more likely to book an appointment a month or so in advance to be physically present. Then, since we are all faithful to our calendars, we tend to keep that commitment.

 ## SCHEDULE BEING PHYSICALLY PRESENT

Pull out your calendar. Pull out whatever it is that connects you to your calendar. Yes, right now, while you are reading this book. (By the way, if you don't, aren't you already conceding to this thing called "in the future?")

Now, look ahead one month. You need to find a two-hour block of time. Two hours. If you can't find a two-hour block of time a month out on your calendar, maybe now is a good time to reassess your priorities, if you truly believe what you have read in this book about the value and impact of being physically present.

Once you find a two-hour block of time, hit that little "schedule an appointment button." In the title section type, "be physically present." Select a two-hour block of time and save that appointment. No need to check with anyone else, it's only your time that you are scheduling.

When that two-hour appointment time arrives, you are just going to be physically present. Between now and then you're going to figure out where to go. Maybe you will go someplace you haven't been in a while. Maybe you will see somebody you haven't seen in a while. Maybe it is a place that you know you should go, but don't want to. Maybe you will stroll down to that block of cubicles where you are not really sure what goes on there. You're not going to prepare a speech. You're just going to show up and talk and listen and be yourself. Be physically present.

That's it! Keep that appointment and then make another one. Repeat this a few more times and soon enough you won't be able stop.

I know leaders who, while they didn't understand the value of being physically present at first, tell me now it's the best part of their jobs.

❑ **Schedule a 2-hour block of time on your calendar to be Physically Present.**

I know leaders who didn't understand the value of being physically present at first, now they tell me it's the best part of their jobs.

An up-and-coming executive on my team had to confront exactly what we just described here.

"I didn't get it," Bruce said. "I didn't understand the value of being physically present in the operations. People would tell me I needed to get out into the field and see what is going on. I didn't take them very seriously. I was thinking, what a waste of my time and the company's time to have me out running around in areas where I had no people reporting to me. My job impacted field operations plenty, but I never got out there to see how."

Bruce found himself in a leadership role in operations. I wish I could say that his new boss encouraged him to get out in the field, but that is not how it happened. His new boss required it. Guess who his boss was? (You guessed it, me.)

"At first I had some serious concerns about being physically present," Bruce admitted. "I don't know those people. What will I do? That's a lot of miles. How much time will this take? I've got a lot of other things that I could be doing. I am very busy now. How can I add this?"

But it started to have an impact on Bruce.

Results From Taking Action

"At first I saw it as a chore, but that started to change over time. I started seeing the value of having those connections with people in the field," Bruce said. "Then when you wanted to change something or effect some change, you could go out and talk to them. It wasn't a corporate guy coming out to talk to them, they had a connection with me."

"When people first meet you and you're a leader from the office, guess what they think?" Bruce asked. "Being present allowed me to establish a relationship. Once I found a reason to be out there, I could tell my story of growing up working hard in a small town and dreaming of doing a job like they do. It is easy to get a connection."

Bruce learned the impact of being physically present.

"Being present allowed me to establish a relationship."

"You don't ever really know how what you do impacts the rest of the people until you get out in the field and see it," Bruce said. "Now I've seen it and that's why I challenge the corporate folks. When we make a decision, we need to know what it means to the people trying to do the work. There are so many other benefits to getting out there and being physically present. It's the thinking time during travel, the relationships you build and the trust you gain. As you build up those connections and those relationships with people, then it's a lot easier to get change done. Yes, even unpleasant change."

"As you build up those connections it's a lot easier to get change done."

Make it Part of Your Routine

Bruce discovered the value of prioritizing.

"I still get all my work done. You figure out that some of what you've been doing that you thought was important is not. You get rid of the stuff that's not as important as being physically present. I used to selfishly travel alone so I could be listening to a book or something like that. Now I travel with other leaders and use that time to keep up on the edges of the business I might otherwise miss. Plus, I am establishing and growing relationships with people."

Bruce gained a lot of wisdom as he made getting out of the office part of his routine, but the real impact showed up during the tough times:

"Now, if I need to make a change or ask them for something difficult, I don't want it to be the first time they see me."

Just Get Out There

Take that two hours you have blocked off and just take some easy steps.

Find somebody who supervises the area you're visiting and ride with them, or walk the plant floor, or sit in with them during their daily meetings. It might freak them out a bit at first, but do it enough, they'll get used to it. In fact, they'll probably start to expect it. Pretty soon, you may find it is the most satisfying part of your day.

Wash, rinse, repeat. Just like anything we want to do well, do it again, right away, before the joy wears off. Most people I know find great value in being physically present and they do it over and over again.

"At first I looked at being physically present as a chore," Bruce now says. "So, I had to force myself out there away from the office. Then, my leadership really started to grow and become more effective. Now I get a real high from it. Actually, I'd give up doing everything else and just go out in the field every day if I could."

"At first I had to force myself out there, Now it is the best part of my day."

Today, Bruce is paying it forward a bit when he runs into leaders who do not understand the value of being physically present. He tells them, "Hey you need to get out more. People used to tell me that I needed to get out more and guess what, they were right."

This simple step of committing your calendar to being physically present is critical.

It simply won't happen unless you start right now.

One of my very first experiences with a true mentoring boss was a fellow named Payton. He was regional president of a major telecom company, and I was the cocky, upstart junior executive under his wing.

Mentors Matter

Change came natural to me; in fact, I got restless when there wasn't enough of it going on. Sadly, I was also too focused on doing what I wanted to do, what came naturally and what offered more immediate rewards. Payton changed that.

Running a multi-state operation, we had a company plane that we used to visit some of the out-of-the-way operating centers. One of those trips was to a switching office in rural Kentucky. The visit was a walk-around—Payton shaking hands, having impromptu talks with a few employees doing their work, maybe dropping by the break room to grab a bite and get a feel for what was on the minds of employees.

The visit was a walk-around, shaking hands, having impromptu talks, dropping by the break room and getting a feel for what was on the minds of employees.

Payton, while not a young man, was fit. He played tennis and golf often and prided himself for staying in shape. Yet, on the plane ride home, I saw him sink into the seat as what almost seemed like a weariness set in on him.

I ventured a question.

"Payton, do you like going out like this?"

He tilted his head my way, offered something of a wink, and said, "It's hard, but they need me to."

I always admired how Payton pushed through his other demands, or time pressures or even his own fairly quiet nature to be out there with the people who were doing the real work of his business. He did it because he chose to do it, and he did it because it was something he committed to on his calendar.

Great leaders schedule time to be physically present.

Great leaders schedule time to be Physically Present.

Chapter 9

Mentally Present Action Plan

Go deep, go often.

Being mentally present means engaging in what is happening at the moment. But being mentally present also means thinking about and improving your leadership. Taking action on this, however, means we actually have to trick our minds a bit.

Here is how it works.

Your mind gives you all the mental power you need to be mentally present and be a great leader. Your mind is hungry, that's why it wanders so often. When your mind is wandering, you are not mentally present. If your mind is hungry, then your imagination is starving. Where your imagination goes to feed, your brain and thoughts will follow. Therefore, leaders need to feed their imagination with the right stuff to pull their minds in the right direction.

Your mind is hungry, but your imagination is starving.

Think of a time when you were really into something, really interested and really stimulated. This is what Hungarian psychologist Mihály Csíkszentmihályi has famously labeled "The Flow." Sometimes we call it The Zone—where we lose track of time and just relish the experience of being totally absorbed mentally in a task, solving a problem or uncovering some new understanding.

At those times, remember how fast you locked in and learned? It seemed like you could do anything! During those times, what do you think that you were stimulating? Sure. It was your imagination. Something captured your imagination, and your attention to detail could not be stopped.

It's hard to focus fully and deeply on a task or an issue when our imagination—or hunger for stimulus—is parked to the side. Don't fight that.

We have to surround ourselves with the elements that ignite our imagination and our curiosity, if we ever expect to use the amazing capacity of our minds to think openly, solve problems or discover new approaches and ideas.

Open Up Your Mind from the Outside-In

How often do you immerse yourself in a book, video or podcast that is just outside of your normal buzz of business? Do you consider that a luxury, a distraction or a necessity?

Each of these mediums serves a distinct and yet common purpose: Books serve as a retreat; podcasts or videos offer more immersive experiences, allowing you to literally hear or see what someone has to offer. But these activities all share the common purpose of allowing us to make learning an intentional part of our lives.

> ## These activities allow us to make learning an intentional part of our lives.

So, how many great books do you read?

I don't mean grazing through on-line articles or news stories, but a book with a singular purpose and message, one that whacks you in the forehead with some idea, theory, perspective or deeper exploration that is different than the everyday diet of information being thrust at us?

The first action step in being mentally present is simply to have a sharp and open mind. We tend to think our minds are an ever-expanding warehouse of knowledge, but biologically we can install a self-closing hinge on that door if we only expose ourselves to reading or experiences that are familiar or comfortable, or that are immediately relevant to something in our lives.

Great leaders understand the imperative to constantly pry open that door. Sure, read your *Wall Street Journal* or some trade publication in your industry, but if you want to be mentally present, stretch your mind by reading things outside of your normal routine and range of vision. Read about great leaders. Read about spectacular failures. Read about the human struggle, the awesome feats. Better yet, don't just read about the Civil War; walk the grounds of Gettysburg. Don't just buy some artwork, sign up for a pottery-making class.

GO DEEP

Commit to reading six books this year that will stretch your mind. Don't have time for that? Then what in the world are you doing that is more important? We're serious. Turn off the TV and pick up a book. Then when you're done with that, pick up another. Make it a habit. Your imagination will appreciate the nutrition.

Note: A quick look at our libraries revealed that the average book is about 200 pages in length. If we can read five pages a day, only on workdays, we will read those six books in a year. Start reading those five pages today!

❑ **Read 5 pages of a good leadership book every day = 6 books in the next 12 months.**

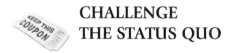

CHALLENGE
THE STATUS QUO

Some of the most revolutionary changes in our world came not from business leaders but from people in all walks of life who thought differently, were willing to challenge the status quo and who rarely had the resources that you have at your disposal within a business. It is the Wright Brothers in their bike shop, Jobs and Wozniac in their garage, Oprah in some modest Baltimore TV talk show studio, Edison at his workbench or Rosa Parks on a bus.

You don't have to be a genius to be mentally present, but you do have to have a sharp and open mind. When was the last time you did something just a little crazy to test your ability to solve a problem? Not a business problem, but how to scale a rocky cliff, or fix something around the house, or take a trip to a completely unknown area, or wander through an art exhibit or museum?

Rather than a vacation to your typical destination of relaxation and comfort, go big and try something you've never done before, where you are out of your element. Trust us, your mind will get exercised as much as your body.

❑ **Try something you've never done before.**

BE A RELENTLESS STUDENT OF LEADERSHIP

Surround yourself with great leadership resources, even if it's only a little each day.

Ken Blanchard says great leaders have an open mind about how they can take in new knowledge about leadership and don't make excuses. Read books, attend mind-stretching leadership workshops, get a leadership coach, whatever works. "It is easy to find a reason that something does not work," Blanchard says. "Learners find what works."

Thinking about yourself or your business in the same way you always have is deadly. Change is essential. Rote thinking leads to rote behavior. Routine breeds complacency. We believe you don't change merely in response to some outside influence or disruption, but you change as a matter of personal discipline. Intentional disruption—a determined pursuit of change—is what invites new ideas.

One of the best ways to expand your understanding of leadership is to take in everything you can—from what you see, read and watch, to what you experience. There is a deep sea of material and insights out there, especially if you are discerning and lock in on a few that really offer wisdom and insight into what leadership really means.

Surround yourself with good leadership material. Sign up for leadership blogs, podcasts, videos and newsletters, along with reading those books. Take eight minutes a day—every day, at the same time each day—to invest in some leadership knowledge with that material. Spend time with your favorite leadership material from the experts you choose. Write down what you took away from that.

This will change your life!

❑ **Surround yourself with great leadership material for 8 minutes every day.**

You can find these great leadership resources yourself, or, I have already done the work for you. Just drop me a note, and I will send you *"Doug's Top 10 Great Leadership Resources"* for free.

Doug@DougSterbenz.com

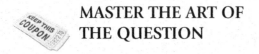

MASTER THE ART OF
THE QUESTION

The ability to think can be a trap if all we are doing is pre-processing what is already in our heads. Being present mentally, oddly enough, requires that we embrace ignorance. Willful ignorance. It wards off the natural tendency to arrive at the easy answer, or the dreaded GroupThink.

Being mentally present means having a keen ability to challenge the status quo. It means interrogating ourselves and our situation to uncover what we don't know.

To challenge the status quo, try to rephrase your statements into questions. "That's the way we do it" becomes an entirely different exercise when it is re-phrased as: "That's the way we do it?"

Being mentally present means having a keen ability to challenge the status quo.

Most leaders would do well to become frequent users of the words *why* and *how* and *what if*. It feels very ineffi-cient; you might even feel stupid. However, the ability to craft a question that invites other views, that jostles you out of complacency, is an exercise in fresh thinking. It's worth it to turn conventional wisdom upside down to see if anything new comes out.

Take an entire day and practice doing nothing but asking questions. It will feel odd at first, and your people might think you have gone nuts, but you'll be surprised how invigorating it can be. It will become a habit. And you will learn something. We promise.

❏ **Spend an entire day just asking questions.**

PAY ATTENTION TO WHAT PAYS YOU

Focus. It's getting harder to do every day, but much like that Amtrak operator, not applying our full faculties to the task at hand can lead to disaster.

Your business should be underpinned by some fundamentals: financial management, having the right customer focus, being able to cleanly execute a pipeline of new ideas and innovations. Being mentally present means fending off the distractions and continually honing your fundamentals.

To use a football analogy, you don't pin your hopes on the Hail Mary pass or dramatic interception, but on how well your line performs. It's not always glamorous stuff, but most often that's how you move the ball in business. You can't get far without it.

As a leader, it is not only your job to focus on the fundamentals, but also to be the voice within the business to make sure others do as well. Doug understood this when it came to his breakthrough record of having no recordable injuries in—of all crazy places—a power plant full of pressurized pipes, furnaces, boilers and massive electrical grids. It came down to the fundamentals.

Write down the fundamentals of your business. It sounds ridiculous, because they are obvious? Try it.

Then ask others. Then compare. Note the gaps. Then, ask yourself and others how those fundamentals can improve every day.

❑ **Write down the fundamentals of your business and ask others to do the same.**

FIRE YOURSELF AND SELL YOUR BUSINESS EVERY DAY

What? We tend to reward ourselves and others for their experience in the business, and that does have value. But the world is changing at meteoric speed, and often the better, sharper skills and insights are outside of our business. If you were to bring in new talent today, wouldn't you expect some fresh perspectives, new ideas and a bolt of energy? As a leader, you need to take that fresh approach every day.

Being mentally present is to put a sharp edge on just how critically we assess the performance of the business. Ask yourself, "If I was an investor, would I buy into the business as it is? If I were to sell it, would I get top market value?" This is not to suggest that your business is just some fungible financial asset out on the sales block every day, but value in our economy is measured by dollars. That is the currency of whether your business is performing well and being a good steward of its assets. If you think critically about where your business is lagging, where assets are not being optimized and where sacred cows are chewing their cud, you will know what to do.

Being mentally present means being just a little restless about how well things are going. Because they can always be better.

Doug and I probably differ a bit on exactly what form this study of leadership should take. I prefer a deeper dive into a singular theme and shy away from the ones that suggest there are "Five Things Successful People Do Before 8:00 a.m.!" In my blogs, I tend to rummage around on a singular topic and tell it in a way that challenges people to consider what they do. I have a good following, but it's not for everyone.

Doug, by contrast, loves those punchy, practical blogs that offer a menu of ideas that people can readily apply. He is a warehouse of those ideas and tips. He tells me those short bits stimulate his imagination in ways that inspire him to go deeper.

Different without a Difference

Our differences, though, are not as important as our shared view that you must open yourself up—continually and determinedly—to resources, perspectives and knowledge outside your normal day. You generally cannot grow on your own, and certainly not as quickly as you will surrounded by good leadership resources.

Constantly seeking out leadership resources challenges us to consider our own leadership style and way of thinking. It may be a bit more osmosis than literal integration, but we do become what we eat. It has been said that you become the average of the six or so people you hang out with the most. If you want to be a great leader, hang out with great leaders—even if that means watching their videos, reading their books or going to their seminars.

To be a better leader, be mentally present.

To be a better leader, Be Mentally Present.

Chapter 10

Emotionally Present Action Plan

Emotions connect people

With your payroll, you can buy their hands. You might even be able to buy their minds. But when we get their hearts, that's when we achieve breakthrough results and set big records. When we are passionate about the work, the workers and the mission, we inspire those around us by being emotionally present.

Being emotionally present takes many forms, including:

→ Being empathetic, caring, vulnerable and authentic;

→ Knowing the role of pride, inspiration, even courage in leading people and igniting their passion for their work; and

→ Being a student of human nature and behavior.

All of this starts, however, with you having a genuine, even boundless, enthusiasm and passion around your business and what it does for others. People are drawn to purpose, to something that excites them, and something that gives them a sense of worth and vigor. That has to start with you.

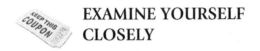

EXAMINE YOURSELF
CLOSELY

Honestly examine yourself and the reasons why you are in your current career. Determine the purpose of your organization and how you fit into that bigger picture. By understanding your role and what gets you excited about your career, you will discover the emotions that inspire you to be a better leader. The point is to dig a bit deeper—below the job description or the annual company strategy or business plan—to get to what leadership author and consultant Simon Sinek famously simplified into "getting to WHY." The answer to "why" contains the emotional presence we must demonstrate to others.

❑ **Answer these questions about your career and where you work.**

Answer the following questions:

1. Why did you choose the profession you are in?
2. What do you see as the larger purpose for your enterprise?
3. What lights you up?
4. Where do you get the greatest satisfaction in what your company does for others?

Leaders should never ask followers to do something they are not willing to do themselves. Therefore, I asked myself the same questions I have asked you to ask yourself.

My Questions

I spent my entire career in some form of the electricity business. Why did I choose the electric business? Why did I get so absorbed with electricity? What made me pick that field?

My Answers

Some people think the electric utility business is boring, simple and unimaginative. However, I believe that I am one of the lucky people in this world who get to provide life-changing electricity to people. What are my reasons?

Electricity is a life-changing product that drastically improves people's lives.

The large-scale equipment involved is interesting, fascinating and challenging.

The people involved in the electric industry are high quality, moral and upstanding citizens.

Does that sound a little too noble or perhaps too distant from day-to-day work? Not at all. In my experience, that larger sense of mission—for me and my people—was the fuel behind our work, the driving force that helped propel us to a much higher level of performance and job satisfaction than if we just looked at the work alone.

Once we understand our own emotional engagement in our work, we need to be able to communicate it to others. By telling our personal stories, we show others the authenticity of our emotions.

To be authentic in our effort to be emotionally present means our personal story matters. People are not as interested or inclined to follow your wisdom and vision unless you are first willing to share the struggle you went through to learn or discover it.

Too often we think it's a little self-indulgent or irrelevant to tell our story, but doing so is what engages people. To first understand your own story, consider following The Hero's Journey:

The Hero's Journey

Life starts in the village, where we are safe, comfortable and perhaps unchallenged.

For Doug, this was helping his dad in the roofing business, with no particular vision for his life. Think of a time where you were just a bit too comfortable with the status quo in your life or career.

The Adventure – something pushes you or pulls you out of the village where the status quo is no longer satisfying, acceptable or even available.

For Doug, this probably started when his father inspired him to go to college and find a better life. Or perhaps his first look at the electric business—that first visit to the power plant—where he started to light up about what it might be like to work there.

Slaying the Dragon – the Dragon is that obstacle, real or imagined, that has to be confronted.

For Doug, it may not have been one event but several that challenged him to step up against the odds and demonstrate leadership. Certainly, later in his career, he had to take some risks—like making the bold statement about safety—that represented times when he had to reach inside himself or reach outside himself for something new or deeper.

The Chalice – the final leg of this journey is to take that transformative experience and share it back in "the village" so others can be inspired and grow.

That is what Doug is doing now with this book.

That may sound corny, but The Hero's Journey has been around since the writings of Homer and is the foundational construct for almost any great movie, play or novel because it speaks to the human spirit for adventure and learning.

Why is taking yourself through this process essential to being emotionally present? Because people are not as interested in what you have to tell them unless you are willing to share the struggle you went through to learn or discover it. Take the time to explore your journey, and you will be on the path to being a more approachable, authentic, empathetic and passionate leader.

CONNECT WITH PEOPLE EMOTIONALLY

As emotionally present leaders, we must connect with people on a human level—and that means emotionally—so here is your assignment:

Take the answers to your questions in the previous action suggestion and build your story around those answers.

Create a two-minute speech on that story. Edit it. Rewrite it. Practice it. (Hire a coach like Paul to help you flesh it out! That's what Doug did. It made all the difference!)

When you are comfortable with your two-minute speech, try it out on some safe people.

Just be your natural human self as you show people why you are in this business and why you love it. Your speech should be the real you, falling in love with your business again and letting others watch.

❑ **Build your story using the answers from the questions above and build a 2-minute speech describing why you love the business you are in.**

TEAM UP

Sometimes when we talk about getting emotional, people look concerned. They say, "I'm not the dramatic cheerleader-type leader. I am not a Rah! Rah! guy or gal. I don't feel comfortable running around giving everybody high-fives at work."

Then we say, "Well, that's because you're probably an engineer or an accountant."
(Hey, Doug is, so we can say it!)

Let's face it. Some of us are just not naturally brimming with emotional presence. The mistake we can make is to think that emotion is only some overflowing fountain of energy. It's not. It is understanding and mastering the ability to connect with people with more than just facts or information. It has to do with pride, encouragement, trust.

If you are struggling with creating your speech, team up. People who struggle with being emotionally present, need to team up with somebody who's better at some of those qualities than they are. Find that person you might find to be annoying. You know the one—always positive about everything and lives to tell you about it. Suck it up and learn from others who have the emotional presence you want. Introverted, non-emotional people tend to only hang around with people just like themselves. Don't do that. Reach out to those extroverts. Set up an appointment and meet with them. They will gladly meet with you, because that is connected with what they live to do. Learn from them.

Emotions do rub off. It may never be your strength, but it is something that you can learn.

❑ **Team up with somebody who's better at emotional qualities than you are.**

Behave your Way to Believing

You have to behave your way to becoming a more emotionally present leader. Your behaviors lead to new habits, those new habits to rituals and rituals to beliefs.

Do you want to get to a point where you truly believe that being emotionally present is a natural part of who you are as a leader? Just like with any skill you have acquired, it is a process:

CHANGE YOUR BEHAVIORS

That may feel really awkward, but try it. The easiest way to get started is to simply express the emotions you feel. Too often we bury them (although they have a way of leaking out anyway!).

TURN THOSE BEHAVIORS INTO HABITS

Once you've learned to articulate or express an emotion, do it again. And Again. Everything in you may scream to go back to your safe place—what I call The Vulnerability Hangover—but keep working at it.

MAKE IT A RITUAL

Start to build your leadership model around integrating emotional presence into who you are and what you do every day. Rituals are ceremonies we take for granted, that have deeper meaning, that we look forward to and don't question. That's where you want your emotional presence to be. Do all that, and you will find that this notion of emotional presence that you once approached warily, is now core to how you lead.

So let's put this into real terms. When you show some emotions, and you get the desired positive result you want, then you become a believer. Once you believe that you are more emotionally present, you will be.

I have worked for all kinds of leaders. I prefer leaders who show their passions openly. Those people are just more inspiring to me. However, I remember one particular leader who at the surface was not very inspirational or emotional, at least not publicly.

Emotional Presence Can Be Quiet

Jim was the first real CEO I worked directly for. Jim is a quiet, mostly introverted, thoughtful man. But he connected with me on an emotional level. He touched my heart. He never said much to me that was directly inspirational. He did his inspiring in a much more subtle way.

Although we achieved numerous goals and had some big successes, Jim never gave the inspirational Rah, Rah speech I so deeply desired him to give. I don't think he ever did that to anybody. I wanted high fives, but there were none to be had from Jim.

One day, I stood in the back of the room where Jim could not see me and listened to a speech he was giving to an important group of people outside of our company. This was a very distinguished audience—other CEOs, public leaders, elected officials—a real VIP audience. To my surprise and amazement, much of that talk was about me and the group I was leading, and he had great things to say. Wow! Jim connected with me that day on a real emotional level without giving a "Rah, Rah" speech or a single high-five!

We must connect with people on a human level; we humans are emotional beings.

Another time, a rather lengthy and hard assignment finally came to a successful end because of the efforts of my team. Though I would have loved to get a high-five from Jim, I didn't stand around waiting for it. Later that week, I received a letter in the mail to my home. My wife opened that letter and when I got home from work, she read it to me. It was from Jim. It has been many years ago, but I still have that letter.

Was Jim a motivating leader? Yes. Was Jim a cheer-leader-type leader, running around the room giving high-fives to everyone on his team? No. Did Jim love the business and let it show? Everybody who knows Jim says yes.

Not everybody will show emotional presence in the same way. But we must *Connect With* and *Connect To* people on an emotional level. You don't need to be the dramatic, cheerleader-type leader running around giving everybody high-fives at work. But as leaders, we must find a way to connect at an emotional level.

We must connect with people on a human level; we humans are emotional beings.

Be real. Be a human being. Be Emotionally Present.

Be real.
Be a human being.
Be Emotionally
Present.

Chapter 11
The Big Day

Make a difference.

The concept of being present as a leader is easy to understand. Maybe even easy to buy into. But buying in and understanding are not enough. You need more than that to make a difference.

The question for you now becomes, "What priority do you place on self-improvement and on organizational learning?"

As a leader, you set the pace and establish the value of improvement in your organization. It is easy to say that you believe in self-improvement and organizational learning, but do you walk the talk yourself?

What priority do you place on self-improvement and on organizational learning?

How much importance do you place on your own self-improvement and that of those in your organization? Are you setting the example by your actions?

My last story for you tells about a time I watched as the value of self-improvement and organizational learning went through the roof.

Skyrocketing Value

Nuclear power plants are large, magnificent industrial facilities. Some pretty important people perform complex tasks as part of their vital jobs there. Those plants generally run non-stop for 18 months and only shut down for refueling outages. On the rare occasion that something happens and forces the plant to come offline and stop producing electricity, it's a bad day.

At one nuclear power plant a few years ago, about 100 of the highest-ranking plant leaders gathered in the training center just two miles down the road from the power plant front gate. These leaders were all there to hear from Bob, an outside leadership expert and trainer, who was trying to help them improve their coaching skills. Rick, the CEO, specifically wanted all the plant leaders to improve their handling of personnel performance issues.

Bob stood in the front of the room and addressed the entire leadership team. About an hour into the training, everyone's mobile phones and message devices immediately began to ring out in unison. Obviously, something of utmost importance was happening at the plant.

The first people to access their mobile devices learned that the plant had just tripped offline. Everybody began scrolling and tapping away at their mobile devices like a bunch of chickens pecking seeds from the farmyard dirt.

Bob looked over at the CEO and said, "Rick, what's going on?"

Rick stood up, went to the podium and said, "Obviously, our power plant has just tripped. Let's take a 10-minute break to check the status of the power plant. Make sure everyone has what they need to handle the situation. Then, in exactly 10 minutes we'll reconvene."

All the leaders went out into the hallway and made their phone calls. Some of them got on landlines and some of them logged on to their laptops. They all did whatever they needed to do to figure out the status of the plant.

Exactly 10 minutes later Rick, the guy who is ultimately responsible for the safety and production of the entire nuclear power facility, stepped up to the podium and addressed the room. Rick outlined the exact status of the plant in the appropriate nuclear jargon that everyone in the room, except Bob, completely understood. Rick then summarized that the plant was offline and in a safe and secure state.

Rick then went on to say in very clear language what would happen next.

"We have very capable people at the plant that have been well-trained to react and handle this very situation. We're going to trust them to do their jobs today, and let them know that we stand ready to assist them with anything they need. We will have a break every hour or more often if needed so we can help if required."

Then Rick continued with the most profound and unexpected words of all, "Our job as leaders in this room today has not changed because of this event. We are here to learn the leadership material that we've committed to learn. So Bob, continue the class, we're all yours."

> ## "Our job as leaders has not changed because of this event. We are here to learn the leadership material that we've committed to learn."

Rick's statement blew everybody away. They all thought that the leadership class would be cancelled and that they were going back to the plant right away.

Higher Value Work

Do you think the people back at the plant heard about what happened out there at that training center? You can bet they all did!

What do you think they thought about the importance placed on leaders to continually learn the skills needed to lead? What about the people in the training room? What do you think they thought about the importance and value of continuous learning? They all knew continuous learning was a part of the mission, vision and values of the organization. I bet they had never before seen a value so clearly displayed, especially the value of continuous personal improvement.

The value placed on continuous learning—in whatever form taken—skyrocketed!

That's where you need to be. As a leader, you set the pace and establish the value of improvement within your organization. You also establish the value of coaching within your organization. Be deliberately present in your own development and the development of others.

Be deliberately present in
your own development
and the development
of others.

Epilogue

It's all common sense, isn't it? This notion of getting out there, thinking of how your business can be better and connecting with your people as a leader and as a person seems so self-evident. Yet it's so easy to forget. We can get so caught up in doing the work that we keep deferring the work of getting better, eventually ignoring it altogether. Everything else is battling for our attention, our energy and our resources.

Inside Track to Action

The reason we co-wrote this book is to give you an inside view of real personal improvement, a game plan to make it happen for you and of the coaching relationship that helped uncover these ideas and put them into action.

We are all personally in charge of our own development. Take action! Go to the Appendix of this book and start checking boxes.

Coaching

We would both agree that a coaching engagement brings accountability, a rhythm and a structure to this process of change. It also brings an interesting discipline. Keeping those scheduled appointments with the coach, even when "the tyranny of the urgent" beckons, is a test of whether you see development—of you and others—as the priority you say it is. Commit to a coaching engagement and you are much more likely to commit to being a good developer of your people, no matter how busy you are.

We obviously believe in professional coaching. One of the goals in writing this book together is to help you get an inside look at what our coaching relationship has been like and how it helped bring fresh perspective to experiences and let them play out in more impactful ways. If a coach is really good, he or she knows how to bring these experiences out and make them a natural part of your leadership style. Frankly, you're kidding yourself if you believe you can do that on your own.

Your Presence Matters

To be present is intentional, and in the short run it can be costly. To put yourself out there in a different way—to engage in conversations with what might be an entirely different motive, to disrupt your own beliefs and understanding about your business, to open yourself up to others and connect on some level other than an operations plan—draws on a different level of energy as a leader.

To be present as a daily discipline, when so many other demands are assaulting your time, is hard. To start being present and to stay present has to be underpinned by a belief.

Just be Present.

To that end, perhaps the most provocative foundation of this book and its premise about being present is this:

None of this makes much sense if you don't believe that the energy, ideas, passion, determination and resolve already exist within your organization, outside of your office.

Everything said in this book is intended to equip you with the tools to unleash the natural pride that people can have in their work, their desire to have their company succeed.

Succeed fabulously.

When you consider who has had the most dramatic impact on you as a person and as a leader, it is almost always someone who was present in the ways depicted in this book.

You won't learn this concept in business school. You may not even learn it later in management training or executive development courses. Oddly, the one "it" factor in leadership—being present, fully invested in the moment—is rarely taught.

If you have been entrusted with leading others, you have your ticket. Sooner or later, your number will be called. Maybe it has been already.

Be Present.

Appendix

Action Plan Checklist

Physically Present:

❑ Schedule a 2-hour block of time on your calendar to be Physically Present.

❑ Show up and just be there.

❑ Repeat often.

Mentally Present:

❑ Surround yourself with great leadership material for 8 minutes every day.

❑ Read 5 pages of a good leadership book every day = 6 books in the next 12 months.

❑ Try something you've never done before.

❑ Spend an entire day just asking questions.

❑ Write down the fundamentals of your business and ask others to do the same.

Emotionally Present:

❑ Answer these questions about your career and where you work.
   1. Why did you choose the profession you are in?
   2. What do you see as the larger purpose for your enterprise?
   3. What lights you up?
   4. Where do you get the greatest satisfaction in what your company does for others?

❑ Use the answers from the questions above and build a 2-minute speech describing why you love the business you are in.

❑ Team up with somebody who's better at emotional qualities than you are.

Share the Message of

"Must Be Present To Win"

To order a copy of this book, visit

Amazon.com

or

MustBePresentToWinBook.com

For bulk copy discounts, email

Doug@DougSterbenz.com

or

Paul@DefiningMoments.me

CPSIA information can be obtained
at www.ICGtesting.com
Printed in the USA
BVOW09s1930040518
515215BV00008B/157/P